AVID

READER

PRESS

100,000

FIRST BOSSES

My Unlikely Path as
a 22-Year-Old Lawmaker

WILL HASKELL

Avid Reader Press
New York   London   Toronto   Sydney   New Delhi

Avid Reader Press
An Imprint of Simon & Schuster, Inc.
1230 Avenue of the Americas
New York, NY 10020

First Avid Reader Press hardcover edition January 2022

AVID READER PRESS and colophon are
trademarks of Simon & Schuster, Inc.

For information about special discounts for bulk purchases,
please contact Simon & Schuster Special Sales at
1-866-506-1949 or business@simonandschuster.com.

The Simon & Schuster Speakers Bureau can bring authors to
your live event. For more information or to book an event, contact
the Simon & Schuster Speakers Bureau at 1-866-248-3049
or visit our website at www.simonspeakers.com.

Interior design by Kyle Kabel

Manufactured in the United States of America

1   3   5   7   9   10   8   6   4   2

Library of Congress Cataloging-in-Publication Data is available on file.

ISBN 978-1-9821-6401-0
ISBN 978-1-9821-6403-4 (ebook)

For my remarkable mom.

Introduction

Five of us sat in a windowless conference room on the fifth floor of the capitol building. The walls were decorated with the sort of soothing, though maybe unsettling, posters you'd find in a dentist's office. And we were making community college free in the state of Connecticut.

"Should free tuition be available to full-time students and part-time students?" Naurin asked. She and the other two nonpartisan attorneys didn't have an agenda to push. They just needed to know what the legislation should say.

I froze and looked at Gregg Haddad, the House chair of the Higher Education Committee. Gregg had been working on this policy for decades, but he was nice enough to treat me as an equal when drafting bills. My toes crunched and my shoes felt too small, like they did when I didn't know the answer on a chemistry test.

Janelle, a policy wonk who always had exactly the information you needed at exactly the moment you needed it, helpfully chimed in. "Including part-time students would dramatically increase the cost of the program," she said.

"Okay, let's stick to full-time students, then," I answered.

"And what about students who already have their tuition covered by scholarships?" Naurin asked.

I looked to Gregg for reassurance. "We should include a stipend to help those students afford books and transportation," he said.

That seemed like the right answer. "That way there's something in this bill for low-income families, too," I added.

"Okay, and age requirements?" Naurin asked. "Is this just for recent high school graduates?"

"No," I answered, my toes finally unclenched. "Let's keep it open to anyone who hasn't gone to college before." I thought about my grandmother, who earned her degree decades after she had graduated from high school. Surely thousands of adults could benefit from a chance to learn new skills at their local community college.

Naurin's questions kept coming, and with each one I started to relax a little bit more. It dawned on me that this meeting was the reason I'd knocked on so many doors, shaken so many hands, and made a very unusual decision after graduation. The pomp and circumstance of being elected into the state Senate had given way to the nuts and bolts of public policy, the details of which would be hashed out today in this drab conference room. Less than a year after graduating from college myself, I was now in a position to help others afford a degree. I didn't have an answer to each of Naurin's questions, but I was figuring out how to think them through, take some chances, and effectively legislate on behalf of a community that had given me this job.

For months, members of my community had doubted if I was really ready to be a state senator. After all, I'd never had a real job before. I was untested and, to some, unelectable. Sometimes those concerns were whispered, and other times they were laid out in the opinion section of the local paper. Most of the time, people's skepticism paled in comparison to the doubt I had in myself. Whereas most recent college graduates were bending over backward to make their first boss happy, I was twisting myself into contortions trying to please 100,000 constituents. They were all my first bosses, and I was determined to demonstrate that they'd made the right choice. Sitting in this conference room, I finally realized that I was up to this job. Because I was doing it.

A few times every month, I get a call on my cell phone from a young person who is thinking about running for office. They share their résumé and describe the values of their future constituents or the challenges facing the zip code they hope to represent. I hear about the terrible voting record of the incumbent they plan to oust—invariably someone who has lost touch with the community and often someone who has held office for longer than this potential candidate has been alive. And they ask questions, both big (Will voters take me seriously?) and small (Who should be my treasurer?). I'm never sure how to respond to either type of question, because the United States has 1,938 state Senate districts, and I only know what it's like to represent one of them. I've noticed, though, that these callers usually tell me that they want to run for office "one day." And every time, I encourage them to rethink their timeline. From the rising cost of college to the rapidly warming planet, the problems our country and communities face are too urgent to only warrant our attention "one day" in the future.

So I find myself telling stories from my campaign and my first year in office. Surely some lessons learned in my tiny corner of my tiny state are relevant elsewhere, and I'm eager to encourage other young people on their own journey to their own statehouse. I talk about hiring my college roommate to serve as my campaign manager, building a bunk bed in our tiny apartment, and then building an unconventional campaign team. I talk about how to decide which houses to approach while visiting your voters' neighborhoods and what to say when someone actually opens the door.

For a generation that came of age as a reality-TV star was elected leader of the free world, young people are surprisingly optimistic about what their future will look like. Sure, Donald Trump's divisive and cruel rhetoric drove many people to look at the government and throw up their hands in disgust. But even (and especially) during the worst moments of Trump's presidency, I'd get that call from someone who was rolling up their sleeves instead. Those conversations left me excited for the next chapter of American politics, because I know that the candidates I hear from are just the tip of the iceberg. Across the country, impatient young people are taking a close look at their representatives and deciding they can do better. They heard President Obama encourage those who are "disappointed in their elected officials [to] grab a clipboard, get some signatures, and run for office yourself," and they're taking him up on it.

This isn't a how-to-run-for-office guide for young people, because I believe campaigns and candidates are too unique to make a book like that useful. Instead, this book continues the conversation I've had with so many other young people who want a seat at the table when public policy is written. In each room where decisions are made, millennials and Gen Z are systematically underrepresented. Every day, policy makers in town halls, state capitols, and Congress decide what the next century of American life will look like, but too often they do so without any input from stakeholders in that future. Representative democracy remains an unfulfilled promise, with white male baby boomers dominating the conversation on both sides of the aisle. Although I don't add much to the diversity of the state Senate, I do bring down the average age by quite a bit.

And for what it's worth, young people have a unique story to tell. We're not a monolith—no generation is. However, we know that climate change isn't an academic problem but an existential threat to our ability to lead happy and healthy lives. We know what it's like to hear a loud noise in the hallway at school and worry about where we would hide if the next Parkland or Sandy Hook took place in our town. We know how hard it is to afford a degree in the twenty-first century.

I wrote this book to nudge those who are on the verge of making that leap of faith to get their name on the ballot. I want to share the highs and lows from my campaign so that hopefully other young candidates can do more and do better. I want to let them in on the stress and the excitement of having 100,000 first bosses, and explain how I learned to be an effective legislator while staying somewhat sane. When more young people take a chance and run for office, our government will spend more time planning for a cleaner, fairer, safer future and less time scoring near-term political points. In short, our representative democracy will come closer to reflecting the priorities of the people it governs.

PART I

1

Extraordinary Problems
and Ordinary People

My name is Will Haskell, and like a lot of young people who grew up bingeing *The West Wing*, I thought I might want to run for office one day. That day felt far in the future, after I'd started a family, maybe bought a home, or at least had a reliable paycheck.

When I was a senior in college, I decided to bump up my timeline. I put my life on hold, moving back to a sleepy suburb after college rather than following my friends to a bustling city. The people I loved thought I was crazy, and many probably still do. But the problems in my state felt urgent. And our politics lacked that urgency.

In my home state of Connecticut, more than 300,000 people live below the poverty line. If I could help to change that sooner rather than later, I saw no reason to sit on my hands until "one day" when I was ready to do something about it. When the Giffords Law Center tells us that one hundred Americans die every day from gun violence, why remain on the sidelines until I was ready to take a risk?

I grew up in a wealthy suburb on the shore of Long Island Sound. My parents divorced after a very short and reportedly unhappy marriage that lasted less than two years, so I was raised on Mondays and Fridays by my single, hard-working mom, on Tuesdays and Thursdays by my unconventional but fun dad, and on Wednesdays by a saint of a grandmother. I alternated weekends between my mom's house in the quiet suburb of Westport and my dad's house in Connecticut's largest city, Bridgeport. I wasn't the senior class president, certainly wasn't the quarterback of the football team, and wasn't involved with the Young Democrats. My friends were the theater kids, and I spent most afternoons in rehearsal for *Into the Woods* or *Avenue Q*. While some of my classmates, especially those who harbored not-so-secret plans to run for office one day, wore suits or at least button-down shirts to school, I wore pajama pants and slippers nearly every day of my senior year. I was a fine student but wasn't at the top of my class. My three much-older brothers, all from my dad's first marriage, had excelled in school and were gallivanting on Ivy League campuses around the time I took my first steps.

My brothers are all kind, successful, and gay (you read that correctly), and those are just a few of the reasons I grew up believing they walked on water. When it came time for me to apply to college, I wrote my personal essay about coming out as straight in a family where gay was the expectation. To my surprise, a Catholic school either thought that was sort of clever or decided to overlook it. So I put all my clothes into a few large garbage bags and headed to Georgetown University. Once on campus, I joined an a cappella group (mainly because my brothers had done so) and volunteered to check coats at some political fundraisers. I sought out unconventional courses, bonded with a few professors, and arranged my class schedule so that I had time to intern on Capitol Hill.

When I entered politics, I learned that the government is filled with people who are similarly ordinary. We need ordinary people—tons of them—to solve the extraordinary problems we face. While too many Americans loathe politicians, there are also too many who deify them, and both extremes fail to capture the reality. Aaron Sorkin instilled in me the belief that the president of the United States should receive a perfect score on the SAT, then juggle multiple games of chess while sorting through an international crisis. Fox News will have you believe that Nancy Pelosi eats children for breakfast every morning. When Barack Obama was awarded the Nobel Peace Prize, he asked, "For what?"

Perhaps our politics would be more functional if we had a realistic expectation and understanding of who represented us in government. Maybe more smart and competent people will decide to run for office if they realize they don't need to be otherworldly brilliant. After all, the last few years have taught me that hard work pays off more than anything else in this job.

I don't have the typical résumé of a candidate for state Senate— no law or business degree, no decades of service on a local board or commission, no spouse and kids to put on a glossy mailer. Come to think of it, I don't have much of a résumé at all. But that's the point. We've been disappointed, for years, by those who conform to our idea of who should run for office. Rather than nominating the same type of candidate again and again, it's time to try something new. After all, we're running out of time to get this right.

2

November 8, 2016

I remember driving to the beach on a clear day in September 2001 to stand with dozens of teary-eyed neighbors and watch smoke rise over Manhattan. My understanding of what our government did next was limited to belting out the Dixie Chicks in the car with my mom, who explained that "Not Ready to Make Nice" was written by a few brave women who opposed a needless war and lost their careers as a result. But I didn't start to care about politics until the era of Barack Obama began.

As my generation learned how to ask a crush on a first date and how to drive a car, Barack Obama taught us how the most powerful person in the world should walk, talk, and tweet. He was the inspiring orator who (virtually) addressed students on the first day of school, and the stoic voice who interrupted my algebra homework to announce that the man responsible for the attacks on September 11th had been killed. His attention to detail taught us the importance of showing up prepared, and the historic nature of his presidency made us feel as though we were living through an exceptional moment in our country's story. Gen Z went off to college feeling hopeful about the future—if occasionally sheepish about that optimism in the face of older, cooler, and more cynical millennials.

I first encountered that optimism in a high school gymnasium on a cold day in New Hampshire. I was eleven years old and sitting next to my dad, a man who follows politics obsessively but solely as a bystander. He's never worked on a campaign, but he's the only person I know who watches all three hours of *Morning Joe*, and he has an unmistakable knack for finagling a front-row seat to history. Dad revered New Hampshire's "first in the nation" primary, and he'd dragged me up to the Granite State for a weekend of political tourism. The way my dad explained it, this was our last chance to witness democracy on the ground floor. We could see major politicians up close, ask them questions, and understand who they are as people. After they win in New Hampshire, they become celebrities, inaccessible to the average citizen.

Sharon, my stepmom, drove us to Exeter, where we scanned the local paper to find each campaign's upcoming stops. We sat down in a living room with John Edwards and shared a coffee with Ron Paul's wife. Although I was only in middle school, I could sense how frustrated these politicians and their staffers felt when my dad occasionally bragged that we were political tourists from Connecticut. They quickly moved on in search of a real New Hampshire voter rather than sticking around for his parental stump speech about democracy on the ground floor.

My dad's carefree attitude came in handy in New Hampshire. When we arrived at Exeter High School on that freezing January morning, we were ushered to the back of the room and told that Illinois's junior senator, Barack Obama, would be speaking any minute. I was relieved to be out of the cold, but my dad had his eye on two seats in the front row. He walked with confidence to the front of the gymnasium and shamelessly gestured for me to join him. I slipped under the rope and made my way to the stolen seats. To my amazement, we found ourselves just a few feet away from the podium. While I thought we'd be arrested any minute, my dad was busy taking in the crowd around us. Unlike every other political photo op we had attended that weekend, this room was filled with young families and students. An enormous poster, plastered above the bleachers, promised "CHANGE" in sloppy blue letters. That word didn't exactly resonate with me, since I didn't know who was in power in Washington and why that needed to change. I knew it had something to do with the Dixie Chicks.

But when Obama took the stage, he spoke with an urgency that was stirring, even to those of us who hadn't been paying attention to politics. Shaking hands quickly with people near the rope line, he seemed like a man in a hurry, both literally and figuratively. I didn't know at the time that he was an underdog, taking on the establishment and being told at every turn that he wasn't ready. But in his speech I heard an insistence that the voice of the next generation wouldn't be cast aside. A few days later, Obama narrowly lost the New Hampshire primary. Despite this setback, his speech echoed the same themes I had heard in the gymnasium. "For when we have faced down impossible odds, when we've been told we're not ready or that we shouldn't try or that we can't, generations of Americans have responded with a simple creed that sums up the spirit of a people: Yes, we can," he said.

Yes, indeed, he did. About a year later, I shook my dad awake when CNN declared that Obama would be the forty-fourth president of the United States. Months later, Dad was breaking the rules again, this time pulling me onto the roof of a porta potty on Washington, DC's National Mall. We held our breath in excitement (and because of the stench below) and caught a glimpse of a forward-looking new president taking the oath of office. Obama's journey to the White House, and the front-row seats that my dad stole for us along the way, taught me that politics was unpredictable, and optimism was popular. Talking heads on television didn't get to decide who was most fit for office. That decision was made by ordinary people who bought blue paint and hung a "CHANGE" poster in the bleachers of their high school gymnasium.

Change came once again on the morning of December 14, 2012. I was eating French fries for breakfast, sitting in my high school cafeteria and racing to finish an essay on *The Great Gatsby*. An alert on my phone popped up, breaking the news about a shooting inside Sandy Hook Elementary School. Newtown, Connecticut, was close by, and the gruesome details spread through the halls of our high school like wildfire. Newtown instantly became the focus of a movement, and the national press soon descended on the quaint town. Our state legislature would later pass a historic gun reform bill, but I spent the day surrounded by students and teachers who were just trying to get through the rest of their classes.

The next morning, our principal came over the intercom to explain the safety protocols that our school had in place. I remember understanding, for the first time, why most school doors were locked, and feeling guilty about all those times I had left the door behind the auditorium propped open for a friend who was late. The school shootings never stopped, but we built up an imperfect immunity to each new tragedy. In fact, the *Los Angeles Times* reported in February 2018 that since Sandy Hook, a gun had been fired on school grounds about once a week. If that statistic seems hard to believe, it's probably because most of these shootings don't prompt alerts on our phones anymore. My high school eventually brought an armed officer into the school, pressured by parents who were focused more on turning schools into bunkers than they were on passing universal background checks.

November 8, 2016, was the moment that transformed our generation from kids into adults. Studying abroad in France that semester of my junior year, I went to bed on Election Night rather than pulling an all-nighter to watch results trickle in from across the Atlantic. When a friend from home called in the middle of the night to talk about Donald Trump's victory, I figured it was a joke and hung up. The next morning, I started doom-scrolling—racing through Twitter to find some bit of good news, only to discover more disappointments.

Obviously, this wasn't the first time a narcissistic and divisive politician would sit in the Oval Office. After all, President Richard Nixon's misdeeds had been recorded on tape and played for the world, dealing a serious blow to the sanctity of the presidency in the eyes of many Americans. But I have to imagine that the average voter hadn't really known who Nixon was when they gave him the responsibility of leading the free world. This time around, we knew exactly what sort of president Trump promised to be. In Evansville, Indiana, Senator Ted Cruz called Trump a narcissist "at a level, I don't think, this country has ever seen." Senator Rand Paul worried aloud on Fox News that Trump would treat the country as his "bully fiefdom." South Carolina governor Nikki Haley told a crowd in Georgia that "Donald Trump is everything I taught my children not to do in kindergarten." Texas governor Rick Perry charged at one forum in Washington, DC, that Trump was "the modern-day incarnation of the Know-Nothing movement." Each of them would later become an ardent Trump surrogate, either serving in his administration or vociferously defending him inside Congress. Cutting taxes for the rich and undermining environmental regulations mattered more than the man's character, it turned out.

Starting with the launch of his campaign on the very spot where President Lincoln had delivered his "House Divided" speech, Obama's presidency was seen by many as a leap forward in the march toward equity and justice. Of course, some of the supporters who I'd seen in the bleachers at Exeter High School had likely been frustrated over the last eight years by the slow pace of progress toward environmental protection, immigration reform, and basic human rights. The Left harbored real concerns over whether Obama had lost his sense of urgency. The crux of these disagreements, though, lay in how quickly to bring about change, not whether or not such change was necessary. Progress felt painfully slow but still inevitable.

But while many of us had grown up complacent that forward was the only direction to move, Trump now promised to put that progress in reverse. To Make America Great *Again*.

None of my French classmates met my eyes on the morning after Election Day. I'd organized many of them to volunteer for the Clinton campaign, taking over the second floor of a local bar so that we could make long-distance calls into Ohio and Michigan. My classmates were skeptical that bothering someone at home would earn their vote (that was decidedly not French), and I worried about swing voters understanding their heavily accented English ("H" sounds are tough, so Hillary sounded more like "Illarie").

Now I was trying to explain through shoddy French what had happened back home, assuring my host family that my real family hadn't voted for Trump. In fact, most Americans had supported the other candidate.

If Donald Trump was going to be in the White House for the next four years, it suddenly seemed critical to figure out who was in power at every other level of government. So, from thousands of miles away, I spent the next few days learning everything I could about democracy outside of Washington, DC. When Obama was in charge, I hadn't cared who was pulling the levers of local and state politics. Now that our federal government was moving in the wrong direction, I became curious about which direction Connecticut was headed, and who was deciding.

I started by looking into Westport's town hall, and I learned that the local officials in my hometown were doing a good job. They were fighting for gun violence prevention, spearheading green energy initiatives, and investing heavily in our public schools. True, the town administration was Republican, but they were mainly keeping the streets plowed and the parks open—not advancing dangerous public policy.

Next, I turned to the state capital. I learned that my state representative, Jonathan Steinberg, championed causes like cleaning up Long Island Sound and improving public transportation. He was a moderate Democrat with a record of success in Hartford, and he'd gotten his start in politics as a dad who attended some Board of Education meetings.

After researching Jonathan, I looked up the next rung of power to my state senator, a Republican named Toni Boucher. Boucher had started serving in the legislature before I was born, and her social media page was filled with warm holiday messages and family recipes. But her voting record revealed that she had spent her career fighting against increases in the minimum wage and reforms to the criminal justice system.

Year after year, she had voted against paid family and medical leave. That made me especially mad, since my mom (like 25 percent of American mothers) had to go back to work within two weeks of giving birth. Since the United States does not mandate paid parental leave, thousands of parents are forced to either give up their paycheck or return to work immediately after having a baby. Our country is a global outlier on this issue, as parents in nearly every other advanced economy are guaranteed some time to bond with their children. With no signs of progress in Congress, some in Connecticut were working to pass legislation to ensure that no one was forced to choose between their family and their career. My state senator stood in the way.

I learned that, in addition to serving in the state Senate, Boucher was running for governor. I raced to finish my schoolwork so that I could watch the Connecticut Republican primary gubernatorial debates over live stream. Far away from Windsor, Connecticut, I watched via YouTube as Boucher told a crowded room that Connecticut had gone "too far" in regulating guns after Sandy Hook. I felt that we hadn't gone far enough.

Fairfield County, often referred to as Connecticut's Gold Coast, is by no means a bastion of liberalism. In fact, the Twenty-Sixth Senate District hadn't been represented by a Democrat in almost fifty years. Once home to George H. W. Bush, Fairfield County has a reputation as a breeding ground for "country-club Republicans" who prefer low taxes and minimal government regulation. Given the extreme wealth of these suburbs, it was hardly surprising that one Fairfield County state senator occasionally used a helicopter to commute to the capital of Hartford. But the culture wars championed by Republicans elsewhere didn't have as much sway in these towns, where most people were pro-choice, supported gay marriage, and didn't lose sleep over the Second Amendment. All things considered, Boucher's voting record felt like a mismatch for the moment. As I fumed about our new president, I channeled my anger into obsessive research about Boucher's votes and public speeches. Donald Trump wouldn't be back on the ballot for another four years, but my state legislators were up for reelection in 2018. And the more I learned, the more I disagreed with the state senator who was representing my friends, my family, and my community. While everyone else I knew was fixated on national politics, my hometown's representation in Connecticut's state capitol seemed like a tangible, solvable problem.

3

Three Job Interviews a Day

I hate coffee. I can't stand the taste of it, nor the haughtiness with which everyone talks about it. But when I came home to Connecticut shortly before Christmas, I asked practically everyone I knew in Westport to grab a cup of coffee. I'd arrive early so that I could order hot chocolate without embarrassing myself, then I sat down with local leaders to learn more about our local state senator. To start, I found out that most people didn't realize she was up for reelection every two years. In fact, I learned that the Democratic Party often had trouble finding someone to run against her. A lot of the people in town seemed to believe that the seat belonged to Boucher by birthright. I wasn't so sure.

Dismayed that no one else was running, I started to think about getting my name on the ballot. Inevitably, I'd come up with a reason not to do it. I probably wasn't old enough (a quick Google search revealed that the minimum age was eighteen). Surely a more qualified candidate would step forward (no one did). As my excuses dried up, it began to dawn on me that running wasn't such an absurd idea after all.

Over "coffee," I laid out the case for why the seat could be won. First, 2016 was an election that flipped all conventional wisdom on its head. Few had expected Trump, a lifelong Democratic donor, to be nominated by the Republicans and to hold the nuclear launch codes shortly thereafter. Second, in that same election, Hillary Clinton had won this district by more than 22 points. Boucher's Senate district encompassed all or part of seven towns, winding from New Canaan, on the southern end, to Bethel, about forty minutes north. Every day, suburbs like these grew more incensed by President Trump's treatment of women and his crass communication style—maybe that anger would also apply to down-ballot Republicans who failed to denounce him. Third, the stakes were too high for Democrats to sit this race out. Connecticut's state Senate was the only tied legislative chamber in the entire country, with eighteen Democrats and eighteen Republicans. Every senator was up for reelection every two years.

I knew enough about politics to understand that the chance to make this big of a difference didn't come along every day. When people think of state government, they probably think of long lines at the DMV or state troopers with funny hats. Those who are interested in politics spend more time tuning in to press conferences in Washington, DC, than they do committee hearings at the state capitol. My dad, for one, drove all the way to New Hampshire to teach me about politics but never spearheaded an expedition to Hartford. However, while much of the electorate isn't paying attention, state policies determine the quality of our public schools, the condition of the roads and highways we drive on, and the purity of the water we drink. In other words, flipping a single seat in the tied state Senate could impact the lives of three and a half million people who live in Connecticut. With Congress gridlocked, states across the country were primed to take up the mantle in the fight for affordable health care, clean government, and voting rights.

Plus, the fact that this seat might be flippable was itself rather remarkable. In most states, local politicians get to draw their own legislative boundaries. In order to establish easy reelection campaigns and strong majorities, they usually draw hyper-partisan districts, where one party has the clear majority of registered voters. Rather uniquely, this district stood a chance of going from red to blue.

I was only a junior in college, and I was thinking of applying to law school after graduation. Maybe I could put that on hold, if I really believed I could be a tiebreaker. I had only recently learned who my state senator was—did I really think I could unseat her? As each of these "coffees" came to a close, I casually floated the idea that, so long as no one else stepped up to the plate, I might run. Many people shook their heads and listed the qualities of an ideal candidate: business experience, PTA involvement, homeowner. Seemingly everyone had some reason why I wasn't the right fit, and why this pipe dream wasn't worth pursuing. That is, until I sat down with Rozanne Gates.

Radiating warmth and filled with stories about protesting during the Bush years, Rozanne put her hand on my shoulder and told me about the discrimination that she and her wife had faced when they had fought for their right to marry. She told me that Boucher had opposed bringing civil unions to Connecticut. She and her wife would help me, she promised. But only if I was in it to win it. I left our coffee with a feeling that running for office might be a risk worth taking, despite the odds of failure. Rozanne's enthusiasm reminded me that I'd meet new friends and make new allies along the way. After all, people like her had been waiting a long time for someone to run.

I had Rozanne's support, but just about every other local Democrat was skeptical. They were certain I would lose, and their greater concern was that I'd embarrass the party along the way. One local politico scoffed in disapproval every time I asked which "Bob" or "Steve" or "Cathy" she was referencing. She was exasperated that I didn't already know the members of the Board of Finance, or the Board of Education, or the Board of Zoning Appeals. I took note of every name she mentioned and soon asked those people for coffee, too.

In no time, my coffee schedule grew like a spider web, and the thought of hot chocolate started to make me sick. In time, I found a coffee shop or diner in each town where I could order tap water without angering the waiters. Sometimes, they'd let me keep a table for hours without moving around for each new meeting.

These coffees started to feel like job interviews, even though I wasn't yet sure I wanted this job, and Democrats seemed only barely committed to nominating a candidate. Every local politico needed to be convinced that I was up to the task, and each one arrived at our meeting with a question or two to stump me. They had the aura of a skeptical boss evaluating a new hire. It occurred to me that answering to all of these people as a candidate, let alone a state senator, would be exhausting.

As I boarded an Amtrak to go back to Georgetown, I suspected that I'd probably forget about this harebrained idea. Campus was filled with distractions, and I'd soon be far away from the diners and coffee shops of the Twenty-Sixth District where I'd set up shop. But throughout the spring semester of my junior year, I surprised myself by tracking bills in the state legislature and keeping tabs on Boucher's votes. College was lots of fun, but the atmosphere was beginning to change, too. More and more, my peers were making plans for after graduation. Many were applying to graduate school, or lining up in the career center for interviews at prestigious consulting firms. To my surprise, my feelings about what to do after college started to revolve around the committee hearings and floor votes in Hartford.

As far as I can tell, there's no tried-and-true way to start running for office. Googling won't reveal step one—trust me, I tried. I was still hedging my bets, filling out law school applications and assuming that someone more qualified would soon announce their candidacy. But every week, I'd call each of the local Democratic Town Committee (DTC) chairs. Those who answered my calls would tell me that no one had stepped up.

I'd figured out during my coffee circuit that the seven DTCs in the Twenty-Sixth District are responsible for deciding whose name ends up on the ballot. These committees are filled with party loyalists who love to retell campaign stories dating back to George McGovern.

They mobilize with equal fervor for presidential contests as they do for planning and zoning elections. Although you wouldn't know it from their sparsely attended weekly meetings or their propensity to misuse "Reply All" on email chains, these committees, and their respective chairs, wield an immense amount of local political power.

To say that the DTC chairs were hesitant to throw their weight behind me would be an understatement.

"Why would you waste your time pursuing a Republican seat?"

"Where are you calling me from? Aren't you still in college?"

The most helpful response came from Alex Harris in Ridgefield, the second-largest town in the district. After listening to my pitch, Alex told me that he'd do everything he could to find a more qualified Democrat to put on the ballot. If he wasn't successful, he'd do everything he could to get me elected. I took him up on the offer, and Alex eventually became one of my most supportive allies.

When the school year ended, I reached out to Jonathan Steinberg, the state representative whom I'd researched many months ago. Whip smart and unapologetically gruff, Jonathan represented Westport in the state House of Representatives. His name came up in nearly every conversation, as many Democrats hoped that he would run against Boucher. Having grown up in Westport, I'd seen Jonathan march in town parades when I was a kid. He had always been dressed in a suit and tie, though he didn't seem to enjoy the handshaking and baby-kissing of local politics. Today, fresh off a softball game with other Westport dads, Jonathan walked into the Sherwood Diner wearing shorts and a short-sleeved shirt.

He wasn't particularly interested in my story about how I became fixated on breaking the tie in the state Senate, nor was he interested in my objections to Senator Boucher's positions. He had served alongside her for almost a decade and knew more about her voting record than I ever would. Unlike the other local Democrats, who wanted to know how I would manage to attend classes in DC while running for office in Connecticut, Jonathan wanted to know my platform.

Surprised but happy to be taken seriously, I started to talk about the fact that commuter trains were slower today than they were in 1950, and why I believed that astronomical student debt was holding Connecticut back. Not one to delay a conversation with niceties or platitudes, Jonathan agreed that these were problems but pointed out that I wasn't offering solutions.

So I shut up and listened as he walked me through how Connecticut could improve train speed by renovating structurally deficient bridges. Then he filled me in on budget cuts impacting the development of renewable energy. He explained the importance of the Long Island Sound Blue Plan, and why declaring water as a public trust was the only way to save our drinking water for generations to come. He dove into the details of state policy, and we started to bond over a shared belief that the right decision and the popular decision weren't always one and the same. Jonathan filled me in on a host of public policy choices that I was embarrassed never to have noticed while growing up here. I took notes as he explained how every other state on the Eastern Seaboard relies on tolls to fund transportation investments, but Connecticut had removed our tolls after a tragic accident in the 1980s. He walked me through the antiquated laws that prevented companies like Tesla from selling electric vehicles in Connecticut. He explained that Connecticut featured 169 towns and no county government, meaning nearly every municipality must pay for its own 911 call center, snow plowing, and other key functions. That sort of economic inefficiency led to higher taxes, and he wanted the legislature to encourage greater "municipal collaboration and cooperation."

"That's sort of a mouthful. Couldn't we just call it regional or county government?" I asked.

"That's what the Republicans call it," he answered. "They paint it as another level of taxation, when really it's a policy to save taxpayer dollars."

This was the first time in the conversation that Jonathan had mentioned politics instead of cold, hard policy, and I saw an opening.

"Why is no one else interested in running for this seat?" I asked. "Why aren't you interested?"

"First of all, I have no desire to drive to seven different towns when I can stay here in Westport," he said. He did look at ease in his hometown diner. "Second of all, the seat isn't winnable. It was literally drawn to ensure that the Republican would never lose."

"But if someone really challenged her on these policy issues, couldn't it be done?" I asked, trying to inspire some optimism.

"I don't think so," Jonathan said flatly.

That was the end of our meeting, and I wasn't sure what to think about Jonathan. He certainly wasn't a power-hungry politician yearning for the spotlight. He was an ordinary person, dedicating his time to public service and trying to solve big and small problems. His fluency with policy had given me a glimpse into all the things I didn't know, and I was resolved to read up on pension debt, tolls, and water conservation. On his recommendation, I started reading everything that the *CT Mirror* published, and when an article seemed relevant to our conversation, I sent it his way. He usually didn't reply, so I was pleasantly surprised when he agreed to get coffee again at the end of the summer. As he walked back into the Sherwood Diner, he was carrying a stack of flyers. They were mailers that Boucher had sent out, dating back several years.

"This is my personal Toni Boucher collection," he said, with the first smile I'd seen from him. "I'm giving it to you, because your campaign needs to call her out on some of this stuff."

"Thank you," I said, more than a little surprised. "I really appreciate this, but I'm still not sure I'm going to run—" He cut me off.

"If you do run, don't shy away from the hard issues," he said. "Voters want honesty. This state doesn't need more meaningless talking points." He gestured down to the stack of mailings. "If you support tolls, get ready to be unpopular."

Forgoing popularity probably isn't the best campaign advice, since local campaigns can boil down to formalized popularity contests.

But Jonathan reminded me that my campaign could stand for something and not just against someone. That made the endeavor seem worthwhile, even if my chances were slim. Before he left, Jonathan wished me luck at school that semester. He gave me his personal email, asking that I stop bothering him with political questions on his government account. I left the Sherwood Diner feeling like I'd already started running.

———

Some candidates have told me that they have a major "aha" moment when they decide to run for office. I didn't. I had a series of "huh" moments, where I learned small but illuminating facts that eventually landed me a place on the ballot. I was inspired by President Obama's farewell address, but I needed to figure out how it might apply to my life. I was angry about Boucher's voting record, but I expected somebody else to run against her. I spent months asking politicians what it would take to throw my hat in the ring, but soon it became clear that I was on my way to becoming a politician, too. I've always hated diving boards, and suddenly I looked down to realize I was standing on one. The only way off was to jump.

I'd spent all summer pretending I was running for office to see how it felt and how others would react. I'd spent months driving to new towns and courting local insiders. But I wasn't fully convinced that I was ready. Now I felt like running was the only choice I had.

4

A Tourist at the Capitol

Before I went back to Georgetown for my senior year, I asked my dad if he wanted to join me for a visit to Connecticut's capitol building. I had never been to Hartford before, and I thought it might be a good idea to see where the Senate actually meets before trying to become a senator myself. When we pulled off the highway and approached the capitol complex, the grandiosity of the place stunned me.

About an hour away from Westport, Connecticut's state capitol sits on top of a hill and overlooks the sprawling Bushnell Park in downtown Hartford. Before the capitol was built in the 1870s, this sunny hilltop was the home of Trinity College. Surrounded by neat landscaping and parking spots that are reserved for powerful lawmakers, the complex still feels a bit like a college campus. The capitol itself looks like a Disney castle, if Disney had built a franchise around politicians instead of princesses. Carvings in gray marble and granite line the building and tell a whitewashed version of Connecticut's founding. The most striking feature of the building is an enormous tower, covered in even more statues, that supports a shining gold dome.

I had imagined that a small state like Connecticut would have a small capitol building. Standing in the shadow of this huge gray castle, I felt absurd for thinking that I could serve in the state Senate. For one thing, I couldn't even find my way inside the building. Although there are doors on every side of the capitol, none of them seemed to open. After walking around the building a few times, we finally figured out that visitors must enter through the Legislative Office Building, a more modern and less intimidating structure built in the 1980s. Connected to the capitol through an underground tunnel and an aboveground skywalk, the Legislative Office Building houses the offices of lawmakers and their staffers, plus hearing rooms, the mail room, a cafeteria, and a gift shop. Built with a marble that emulates the capitol, the building's six-story open-air plan imposes a radical transparency on the lawmaking process. From almost anywhere in the building, you can see who is huddled with whom, and who is waiting outside which office.

Right when we walked in, a woman in a red blazer offered to give us a tour. As an intern in Washington, DC, I had given dozens of tours of the U.S. Capitol Building. But those were always arranged months in advance, so I was surprised that someone sitting at the front desk was willing to drop everything and show us around. She introduced herself as Ms. Ellaneous, which made my dad laugh, and she explained that she worked for the League of Women Voters. As we made our way into hearing rooms and through the gift shop, we realized that dropping everything may not have involved dropping very much at all. The building seemed abandoned, with only the occasional staffer wordlessly passing through the halls. Ms. Ellaneous explained that the legislature meets for only four to five months a year, and the building is pretty quiet during the off-season. While staff members continue to answer mail on behalf of their bosses, the legislators return to their districts and fight to get reelected.

I'd never considered the fact that state senators have a staff. If I ran and won, who would want to work for a twenty-two-year-old senator? We continued along the tour, traveling via tunnel to the capitol building itself. As we walked by the offices of the secretary of state, the lieutenant governor, and the governor, Ms. Ellaneous spoke about Connecticut's role in the Revolutionary War and pondered whether or not state hero Nathan Hale really spoke the famous words, "I only regret that I have but one life to lose for my country." She told the story of how an enormous statue sitting in the rotunda was originally sat atop the dome.

But I couldn't concentrate on any of that and instead guided the conversation to the daily mechanics of the legislature. Why did some legislators have offices in the capitol? Those were reserved for leadership, I learned. Why were there rope lines everywhere? Connecticut has strict rules about where lobbyists and members of the public are allowed to stand when the legislature is in session. I found out that many areas are kept clear for lawmakers to move quickly around the building without being harassed.

As we entered the House of Representatives, Ms. Ellaneous explained that Democrats sit on the right and Republicans sit on the left. The strikingly bright room is jam-packed with desks (151, to be exact). I scanned the chamber to find Jonathan's seat, and I wondered about trivial things like what he kept inside his desk, and whether or not he liked the people who sat beside him. When we made our way to the third floor, where the Senate sits, I became concerned that we might run into Senator Boucher. Stupidly, I asked if the Senate was voting on anything that day.

"Not today, not tomorrow. Nothing until February," our guide reiterated, with a hint of annoyance that she had already covered this. My worry was ridiculous anyways—Boucher had no idea who I was. On the third floor, we encountered a room blocked off for "Senators Only," which predictably piqued my dad's curiosity.

"What do you think happens in those rooms?" he asked me, reminding me of Grandpa Joe walking around Willy Wonka's Chocolate Factory. Ms. Ellaneous assumed the question was for her, and she explained that senators spend hours sitting in those caucus rooms, eating together and discussing each bill before it receives a vote.

"No one goes in those rooms except for senators and their top staff," she said. At this point, my dad's temptation was bubbling over. On the drive up to Hartford, I had made him promise that he wouldn't tell anyone about my plan to run. I shot him a quick glare, reminding him that not even our new friend Ms. Ellaneous could know.

"Sounds like a fun job," he said with a smirk. On the fourth floor, we entered the Senate gallery and looked down at the chamber. Unlike the House of Representatives, this room was strikingly empty. The desks of thirty-six senators were arranged in a circle, not by party but by district. At the front of the room stood a podium for the lieutenant governor, who also serves as the president of the Senate.

"That isn't just an honorary job, like the vice president serving as the president of the Senate in Washington, DC," our guide explained. "She presides over the Senate just about every day they are in session."

Ms. Ellaneous told us that the chair behind the podium was carved from the original oak tree in which Connecticut's charter was hidden from the British in 1687. She proceeded to tell us that no one is permitted to step on the white seal that sits in the center of the room's red carpet. I nodded politely but was laser focused on Senator Boucher's seat. I couldn't take my eyes off the placard in front of her desk, and then her name on the gigantic voting board.

"Can you imagine pulling this off?" I whispered to my dad as we left the gallery.

"It would be something," he said.

———

I returned to Georgetown with my determination to win redoubled. Whether pacing around my apartment or walking to class, I developed a reputation for having a phone glued to my ear. I called the DTC chairs almost as often as I called my family, constantly checking to see if someone else had thrown their hat in the ring. I called statewide party officials and left messages about why I thought a historically red seat could be the key to breaking the tie, and why they ought to invest in winning this district. Sure, the Twenty-Sixth District hadn't been represented by a Democrat since the 1970s. But whispers were starting about a blue wave taking shape in response to President Trump's election. I reached out to gun violence prevention activists to enlist their help, recounting Boucher's declaration that Connecticut had gone too far in regulating guns. I stepped out of a cappella practice to speak with state representatives who were nice enough to fill me in on where Connecticut stood when it came to cannabis legalization or access to reproductive health care. Maybe it was because the election was growing closer and no one was stepping forward, or maybe it was because my youth wasn't as glaringly obvious over the phone, but for whatever reason, the politicos I spoke with were increasingly supportive. I learned how to do more listening than talking, and how to condense my scattered thoughts into a short elevator pitch. And at the end of every conversation, I asked for more people to call.

5

Onboarding the Cion House

Some conversations required more than an elevator pitch. I was driving my girlfriend, Katie, home from a date when I told her about my idea to run for the state Senate. Focusing on the road gave me an excuse not to watch her reaction. We were hoping to live in the same city after graduation, and this would certainly put a wrench in those plans.

Katie and I met when she was my lab partner in physics during our senior year of high school, and as we learned about friction and gravitational pull, I became enamored by the way she thought. She was the most well-read person I'd ever met, and was always ready with a witty joke or jab. She was friends with the popular crowd, whereas I spent all of my time after school with the Staples Players, our school's theater group. Over the course of our senior year, I drafted our lab reports and watched Katie rewrite them. I saw her grow tired of high school cliques and endless talk about prom after-parties. I read along as she steered the school newspaper, on which she served as editor in chief, away from fluff stories and toward substantive journalism. I learned that her father had passed away when she was young, and I bought her a Carvel cake when she got into Princeton, her dad's alma mater.

Katie is and was a better writer than I am, so when I decided to write an article about cyberbullying in our high school, she ghost-wrote all the best lines. She had a talent for putting privilege into perspective, replacing my dry explanations about Westport's median income with the observation that "we don't walk through metal detectors on our way to class, and the main job of our school 'security force' is to hand out tickets when students' Jeeps and Audis park in staff parking spaces." Witty, self-effacing, and quintessentially Katie.

One day in physics, I asked Katie what she had planned for her senior internship. Our high school cleverly distracted second-semester seniors, otherwise prone to disrupt or disregard class, by giving them internships and making them someone else's problem. Katie was planning to intern at a local tutoring company, where she would help administer practice SATs. I begged her to apply instead for an internship on the reelection campaign for Congressman Jim Himes, Fairfield County's voice in the U.S. House of Representatives. We carpooled to the interview together, and she was horrified when I changed into nicer pants in the parking lot before the interview. We both got the job.

We started driving to work together, then kept each other company running errands after work was over. One afternoon while we jointly worked through our to-do lists, I got a text from a parent who was very involved with the Staples Players.

"Are you coming??" she wrote.

"Shoot. I'm so sorry. Yes, on my way," I wrote back. I'd completely forgotten that the Board of Education was soliciting public comments on a proposal to cut the theater budget. As the president of the theater group, I had promised to speak out against any cuts at the meeting. I asked Katie if she would come with me, although she didn't have much of a choice since I was her ride home.

Arriving thirty minutes after the session had already started, we quietly took seats in the back of the room. I noticed that a tall woman sitting beside the superintendent made direct eye contact with Katie when we walked in. Katie, with characteristic nonchalance, whispered that her mom, Marge, was sort of a big deal at town hall. In fact, she'd written the budget I was about to criticize. I felt a pit in my stomach.

"Why are you here??" Marge texted Katie.

"My friend Will is mad about the budget," she responded. Marge rolled her eyes, and any hope of dating Katie suddenly threatened to slip away.

Suffice it to say, Marge and I got off to a rocky start. But once I started dating her daughter, we became unlikely friends. I learned why she had made modest cuts to the theater budget, and she understood why I protested against it. Marge was pragmatic through and through, and she reminded me of my mom as she juggled work and family. I learned that Katie came from a political matriarchy. Her great-grandmother, Marion Newberg, had served as the campaign manager for Ella Grasso, Connecticut's first female governor. Although Marion had always wanted to run for a seat in the Connecticut House of Representatives, she was dismissed by the fraternity of local DTC chairs. Her daughters, Devra and Esther, carried on the family tradition. Esther became a key player in numerous presidential campaigns and rose through the ranks on Capitol Hill. Devra served for years as the chair of the Board of Education in Vernon, Connecticut. Devra's daughter, Marge, became chair of the Westport Board of Education. In fact, Katie has distinctly negative recollections of posing for campaign photos and joining her mom to meet commuters at the train station.

Marge was a political force in town, though she hated a lot about politics. In fact, she so despised schmoozing that when she served on the Westport DTC, she would sit in the party headquarters and repeatedly call her own house instead of dialing prospective voters.

As I fell in love with Katie, I also grew to enjoy spending time with her family. I learned that mayonnaise was a monstrosity forbidden in their home, and no one held grudges. Screaming at the top of your lungs over a missing pair of flip-flops at 6:45 p.m. wouldn't get in the way of a perfectly amiable 7 p.m. dinner. Dark humor prevailed; I'd squirm when they laughed that "you can't spell dead without dad."

Unlike me, Katie makes decisions slowly and deliberately. She doesn't like to be rushed into any position. In fact, one of her biggest pet peeves is that I often ask whether or not she liked a movie as we walk out of the theater. She wants time to reflect—a foreign concept for me. So it came as no surprise that her reaction was muted when I told her that I wanted to run for the state Senate.

"Don't laugh, but I think I might want to run for office after graduation," I told her as we made our way down the Post Road.

"What? Where?"

"Here. Westport's represented by a Republican state senator, and I think she's beatable."

"I'm not moving back to Connecticut," was her first response.

"I know. I'm not even sure about this yet. But no one else is running."

"There's got to be someone more qualified."

Katie's reservations were reasonable, and we both wondered how much longer we could manage long-distance. But as we drove through town, I explained how I'd become interested in the race, and what it would look like to actually run for office. I talked about the issues I wanted to campaign on, and how I'd probably lose and could then apply to law school afterward. Katie remembered that her older brother had interned for Boucher when he was in high school. I didn't know where she stood on the issue by the time we pulled into her driveway.

But when we got inside, Katie told Marge that I was running for the state Senate.

"Well, I was thinking of running against Toni Boucher," I clarified. "I know it's a long shot—"

"Do it," Marge interrupted. I was surprised by her reaction, but she knew all about Boucher's voting record.

Marge even offered to be my deputy treasurer as she chopped

brussels sprouts in the kitchen. The treasurer's name is printed on every flyer, providing an opportunity for unknown candidates like me to gain credibility and associate myself with someone more popular. The deputy treasurer doesn't have a public role, but they do the grunt work of opening a bank account and filing away receipts. Marge didn't consider herself qualified to be the treasurer, which epitomized her humility. "I'll keep track of donations and expenses," she said, "but you need someone as treasurer whose name will boost your campaign." Then Katie chimed in.

"My mom should be the treasurer," she suggested. I immediately agreed. Although she may not know it, Marge was respected in town and would lend all the credibility we needed. Second, Katie's suggestion meant she was on board with my idea to run for office. There's no way she would volunteer her mom to help a campaign she thought was pointless. Over dinner, we started to lay the groundwork for what needed to happen next.

6

Picking a Campaign Manager

J ack Lynch and I met at a summer camp in upstate New York when we were both eleven years old. Neither of us remembers too much about the other, and most of my recollections from that summer involve swimming in a freezing lake, figuring out how to use a lacrosse stick, and learning a host of other things that didn't come naturally to me.

Six years later, Jack sent me a Facebook message and reminded me that we had met at Camp Dudley. He, too, was headed to Georgetown in the fall, and he suggested that we pair up as roommates. Soon thereafter, he arrived at Georgetown with his mom, dad, and the same black trunk he had used at camp. He hung the flag of his New Jersey prep school on the wall and seemed like a pretty conventional Georgetown student. At least comparatively.

I arrived at school with my mom, grandmother, dad, stepmother, and her dogs, all of whom crammed into our tiny room on the second floor of a freshman dorm. Jack's family followed all the rules, moving in during the precise window that the school had recommended. My mom and I snuck into the dorm the night before, borrowing a janitor's rolling garbage bin to haul around the garbage bags I'd filled with clothes. Jack's goodbye with his parents was quick, uneventful, and Irish-Catholic. When it came time for my mom to say goodbye, she sobbed and threw herself on the hood of the car.

Although our families were different, Jack and I actually had a lot in common. We both arrived that fall with a long-distance girlfriend whom we had met in high school. We both wanted to work in politics one day and signed up to major in government and minor in journalism. We each joined campus organizations that made the other roll his eyes. Jack became a leader in Hoya Blue, a group that hyped up the student section at basketball games. I joined the Georgetown Chimes, an a cappella group that sang the national anthem at said sports games and usually left after the first quarter.

The first month of college can feel like speed dating as you balance a fear of sitting alone with an exhaustion of small talk. As we met others in our dorm, Jack's ability to judge a person's character was immediately apparent. He could discern who was smarter than they let on and who pretended to know more than they did. He figured out who was genuinely interesting and who had memorized a few fun facts about themselves. If I occasionally brought Jack out of his shell, he kept me from getting into any trouble. He made sure we went to the National Mall to see the pope, and I made sure we had costumes ready for Halloween.

We got along so well that we continued rooming together our sophomore year. In the spring of our junior year, I told him about my idea to run for the state Senate, and he was understandably skeptical. He asked all the right questions, both personal and political. What about law school (not sure), and what about Katie (she's in)? How close did the Democrats come to defeating the incumbent in previous elections (not close), and how had Trump performed in the district (he lost by 22 points)?

Jack hadn't grown up in Westport, but his hometown of Westfield, New Jersey, wasn't all that different. He watched the news as closely as I did, and he believed that young voters and suburban women could play a big role in the midterm elections. While waiting in line at the Tombs, Georgetown's college bar, we'd talk about which towns were winnable and which issues were salient. Could we get people to care about voting rights? Was it worth it to spend time campaigning in a deeply conservative town like New Canaan?

We also talked about his postgrad plans. He was busy applying to congressional campaigns that seemed critical to Democrats winning control of the U.S. House of Representatives. Our roommates, most of whom were heading to fun cities on either coast, asked if he was really willing to move to Iowa or Arizona to knock on doors. I trekked home to Connecticut more frequently; he sent out his résumé across the country.

So far, running for office was a one-man operation of dogged phone calls and probing hot chocolate chats. Eventually, I knew that a serious campaign would involve larger events, offices to staff, and maybe even volunteers to manage. In other words, I couldn't handle this all on my own. One day, I stopped by the office of a professor whom I considered a friend. Professor Ungar, or Sandy as he allowed students to call him, was ecstatic when I shared my plan to run for the state Senate. We chatted about the issues I'd run on, and whether or not I had any embarrassing photos up on Facebook. As I stood up to leave, he asked who was going to manage the campaign.

"I haven't thought about it much, to be honest," I said.

"Pick someone you trust," he told me as I left.

That afternoon, I called everyone I knew in politics. I started with Maryli Secrest, my former boss on the Himes campaign. I remembered Maryli to be a frighteningly hard worker, pacing around the office barefoot while shouting into a speaker phone. She was ruthless at cutting budgets, believed in data above all else, and relished the game of politics. These days she worked as a political consultant for candidates across the state. I knew I wanted Maryli on board, but she wouldn't have time to manage this race. She passed along a few names, each of whom I called right away. They were all friendly and brimming with useful insights. But with Sandy's words echoing in my head, I wasn't sure that I really trusted any of them.

Whether he liked it or not, Jack overheard all of these conversations. I pace obsessively when I'm on the phone, and I walked in laps around our small apartment while talking to potential managers. When Friday finally arrived, Jack and I joined some friends for a drink at the Tombs, which was dangerously located right across the street from where we lived. When we sat down at the bar, I vented about the awkward conversations with potential campaign managers, and Jack complained that he hadn't heard back from any campaigns yet. Suddenly it clicked.

"Why don't you manage my campaign?"

"I thought you'd never ask," he said. We both breathed a sigh of relief before diving into the details.

I warned him that it wouldn't pay much, and he'd have to live in Connecticut after graduation. I promised that we would be equal partners in running this campaign, and we'd do things differently than the candidates who had previously lost to Boucher. Jack had never worked on a campaign before, but what he lacked in professional experience he made up for in experience dealing with me. Since move-in day of freshman year, we'd come to understand how the other thought about politics and people. Jack understood my fear that our campaign would become a laughingstock. I understood his need to bring order to chaos, and saw his potential to make a haphazard campaign a bit more organized. I knew about his inability to do work after 9 p.m., and he knew about my inability to spend more than an hour by myself. Having lived together for years, I knew I could trust him with every aspect of this campaign. Jack knew that I wasn't running to make a point—I was running because I wanted to win. I'd come to believe that with a well-run campaign, there was a narrow path to victory next November.

7

No Minimum Age to Being
on the Right Side of History

Marge, Jack, and I made for an unconventional team. Jack was intimidated by Marge, and I wasn't exactly eager to give any orders to my girlfriend's mom. Although we all got along, Marge was undoubtedly in charge. She opened up a bank account, and now it was our job to fill it.

In most states, I could never afford to run for office. The loose campaign finance regulations that pervade our political system at every level disproportionately benefit those who are independently wealthy and can spend a small fortune financing their own campaign. Candidates who are well connected can tap into a circle of wealthy colleagues and friends as they launch their campaigns. That helps to explain why the typical congressional representative has a net worth of $500,000, or roughly five times the median US household net worth. One reason why our democracy isn't representative is that most people just can't afford to run for office. Consequently, women, people of color, and younger generations are absent from most of the rooms where decisions are made.

Connecticut offers a glimmer of hope. After a Republican governor's political scandal in 2005, the state legislature created the Citizens' Election Program (CEP), a form of public campaign financing.

Instead of requiring candidates for office to raise money on their own (giving the wealthy an advantage and leaving everyone else in a rut), the CEP gives a lump sum to candidates who demonstrate genuine public interest and support.

Marge, Jack, and I needed to raise only $15,000 in order to prove that we were a real and legitimate campaign. Once we did so, we'd receive a more significant grant from the state. Most importantly, that grant was exactly equal to the grant Boucher would receive. Remarkably, an unlikely challenger and a deeply entrenched incumbent would have the exact same amount of money to spend. Three hundred of the donations had to come from people who lived in the seven towns I was hoping to represent, and no donation could be larger than $250. I'd never done any fundraising before, but this seemed doable. It boiled down to asking 300 people for $50.

Even under these uniquely egalitarian circumstances, we had plenty of questions. How, exactly, do we collect the money? Was it possible to start fundraising while I was still in school? To kick off the campaign from hundreds of miles away, we decided to film an announcement video. Unable to pay professional ad makers, I called a friend from high school who had recently started a production company with her girlfriend. Alex and Quinn had never made a political video before, which I thought made them the perfect team to help launch this unusual candidacy.

One cold winter day, the three of us piled into a car and drove around the seven suburbs included in the Twenty-Sixth District. The major highways in Fairfield County run east-west, but this puzzle piece of a district extends north-south. So driving from town to town requires navigating a maze of winding and narrow back roads. Most people who live here commute to offices outside of the district, driving an average of thirty-eight minutes to and from work each day. There's lots of beauty inside the 142 square miles of the Twenty-Sixth District, including sunsets over Long Island Sound and waterfalls along the hiking trails in Redding. There are also strip malls and cul-de-sacs that could easily be copied and pasted from any suburb in America. The median age in the district is forty-four, and 41 percent of households have an income higher than $200,000. Countless streets of single-family homes are interrupted by quiet Main Streets, nine train stations, more than a dozen churches, four synagogues, one Hindu temple, and one Tibetan Buddhist Center for Peace. Taxes are low, property values are high, and the top-ranked public schools draw families who are eager to give their children a good education. Still, the most striking feature of the Twenty-Sixth District is the absence of development. Hundreds of acres of forests, preserved as open space, cover 28 percent of Ridgefield and roughly the same percent of Weston. As Ridgefield's first selectman boasted in one campaign ad, his town has great schools and a historic main street, but also a whole lot of "nothing at all."

Alex, Quinn, and I didn't know much about these towns outside of Westport, but we tried to find filming locations that might be recognizable to those who lived there. We drove to Putnam Park in Redding, zeroed in on a downtown gazebo in Wilton, and stood outside the supermarket in Weston. In between stops, I changed clothes in the back seat of their car so it wouldn't be obvious that the ad was filmed on a single day.

Alex and Quinn also wanted B-roll. B-roll, I learned, is a series of shots that can be spliced throughout the video, breaking up the boring visual of me staring into the camera.

To fill these shots, I asked my family and friends to sit with me and smile, or walk with me and nod. My grandparents invited a half dozen of their friends over, and I sat with them to explain why I was running for office and why it didn't matter what we said, since B-roll has no sound. I shook hands with Katie's twin brother at the front door of their house and walked along the New Canaan train tracks with one of my roommates at Georgetown.

I received the first cut of the video two weeks later while Jack and I were sitting, once again, at the Tombs bar. Although the video had no sound yet, we played it over and over again. We showed it to friends, who gave us a thumbs-up before ordering another drink. We showed it to the bartenders. For the first time, the campaign felt real.

Before we released our first ad, Jack realized that he'd better tell his parents about his postgrad plan. He wanted something concrete to show them, probably so that his new job seemed slightly less risky. In other words, he needed a contract. Marge and I had no idea what a campaign manager's contract should look like, and it became increasingly clear that we had a host of other questions about basic campaign infrastructure. We needed someone who had been through this before. We needed Maryli.

Officially bringing Maryli on board was a no-brainer, since she'd been informally advising me for months. She knew the nitty-gritty details of how to run a campaign, and she somehow brought both order and chaos to our conference calls. Chaos was a part of the deal, because I was just one of the many candidates whom Maryli was advising. She didn't have the time to put out every fire or draft every press release, but she could identify shortcomings in our campaign and think through our field strategy. She wanted concrete fundraising deadlines and a data-driven volunteer plan.

To this day, I have no clue how old Maryli is. Oftentimes, it felt like she was our age. Short in stature and often wearing a flannel or sweatshirt, she crisscrossed the state with a messy car and broken windshield wipers that she never bothered to fix. She made sure there was room in the budget for junk food in the office, traded gossip during late-night drinks, and pulled all-nighters when one of her campaigns was in crisis. Other times, she beamed with pride about her son, laughed when we didn't know how to balance a checkbook, and waged an expletive-filled war with a vendor who hadn't delivered lawn signs on time. On those days, I'd remember that she was the only real adult in the room. And as such, she was always pretty candid that she didn't think our race was winnable. She liked me, but she had a hard time imagining a college student beating one of

Hartford's most deeply entrenched incumbents. Luckily, that didn't stop her from imposing some message discipline.

On a blank poster board, she introduced us to the messaging square. Divided into four boxes, it asked four basic questions: What do I say about me? What does my opponent say about me? What do I say about my opponent? What does my opponent say about herself?

Maryli watched our announcement ad and wondered aloud what we were saying about me. First of all, I wore a suit and tie in almost every shot. I had hoped this would convey that I was serious and professional, but Maryli let out a big belly laugh and said that I looked like a middle-school student trying on his dad's suit. She liked the shots from my grandparents' living room, which synced with the voiceover, "I know what this district cares about, I know what it worries about, I know what it wants to pass down to future generations."

But did I? In a shot from the Westport train station, I narrowed in on transportation improvements. Since thousands of my neighbors commuted to work in Manhattan, this was sure to resonate. But I also spent much of the video talking about voting rights and criminal justice reform, two issues that mattered to me but probably didn't cause too many suburban voters to lose sleep at night.

What did I say about my opponent? I came out swinging, more aggressively than Maryli would have liked. Less than thirty seconds into the ad, I charged that "we're a levelheaded district, and yet somehow our state senator is complicit in the Republican Party's turn toward extremism." Those were admittedly harsh words to describe a senator with a modest record of bipartisanship, and Maryli raised her eyebrows. She was probably right that asking voters to take a chance on a college student over someone they had supported for years required a bit more tact.

What did my opponent say about herself? Boucher was certainly going to run on her legislative experience, so poking holes in that record made sense. I let viewers know that she had voted against paid family and medical leave, hoping that would piss off a lot of parents in our area who had struggled to juggle a family and a career.

What did my opponent say about me? Well, nothing yet. But we didn't need Maryli's expertise to predict the eventual attack—I was still in my first year of legal drinking. Was I really ready to determine what level of taxation was appropriate for corporations and families to pay? The best answer, unexpectedly, arrived during a graveyard shift at Hoya Snaxa.

Since my first semester at college, I'd worked in a convenience store called Hoya Snaxa (a play on Georgetown's unofficial Latin motto, *Hoya Saxa*). Snaxa, as we called it, was a source of steady income and endless entertainment. We blasted music while stocking the shelves, experimented with flavors in the Slushie machine (they all tasted like sugar), and hunted the mice that ate into our profits. The only downside of the job was working a closer on the weekends. As the director of personnel, I got stuck with those shifts every few weeks. On the bright side, the time passed quickly when dealing with a crowd of late-night snackers, and it provided the chance to bond with a fellow cashier while you watched drunk shoppers clamor for Easy Mac and ramen.

One night, I was working a graveyard shift with Felix, a sophomore who was new to the store. Aside from my roommates and my favorite professor, I hadn't told anyone on campus that I was planning to run for office after graduation. But Felix and I didn't know too many people in common, and I figured that he wouldn't leak the news to the Connecticut press.

"Felix, did I tell you I'm running for the Connecticut State Senate?" I asked, knowing the answer was no.

"Bullshit."

I had good reasons for avoiding this exact conversation. If I said it quickly, my postgrad plan sounded absurd. If I provided more details about how I came to the decision, I wound up subjecting an unsuspecting classmate or coworker to a detailed conversation about the shifting politics of southwestern Connecticut. It wasn't a casual and fun party exchange:

"I just signed my offer from Deloitte. What are you doing next year?"

"Going home to run for the state Senate against an incumbent who's been in office longer than I've been alive."

"Huh?"

Everyone who I told thought I would lose, and I didn't have much evidence that they were wrong. But Felix didn't need much convincing.

Without looking up, he shrugged and said, "There's no minimum age to being on the right side of history." That had a nice ring to it, so I jotted it down as a note in my phone. The more I thought about his point, the more I realized that it summed up our campaign. This was a historic opportunity to stand up to the Trump administration on the state and local levels. Yes, I was young, and no, I wasn't trying to hide it. You don't need decades of legislative experience to believe that every student should feel safe in the classroom, or that the train to Manhattan should be faster than it was in the 1950s. You don't need the perfect résumé to stand up for a more decent government—you just need to decide that you're willing to do it.

"There's no minimum age to being on the right side of history," was our answer to everything my opponent would say about my youth. She could attack me for my age, but we embraced it.

With Jack, Maryli, and the videographers on board, our team was growing. But I still needed money to pay everyone. On Thursday, March 1st, from our dorm room, we released our campaign video, website, and social media pages simultaneously. Most importantly, we started asking for donations.

Maryli recommended that I do a few hours of "call time" later that week. Call time involved sitting down and calling everyone in your contacts to ask for money. Infamously, it requires you to put your family, friends, and friends of friends on the spot, soliciting the credit card numbers of people you love and people you barely know. It's the worst. Luckily, the response to our video was stunning. Along with positive comments and words of encouragement, money started flowing in from back home at a rate we didn't anticipate. Friends from elementary school, teachers from high school, and hundreds of people I had never spoken to donated between $5 and $250. I was amazed that so many people believed in this campaign. As each donation came in, I breathed a small sigh of relief that, instead of watching the video and laughing, people decided to open up their wallets.

That night, Jack and I hosted a campaign kickoff in our dorm. While I was in class, my roommates printed out copies of our campaign logo and used painter's tape to sketch a huge "WH 4 CT" on the wall. Jack set up two laptops upstairs for people to plug in their donation information. When I got back home, I couldn't believe that they had done all of this for me. Our roommates weren't a sentimental bunch, but they had transformed our apartment to show their support. They had even found a blank poster board and drew a big thermometer. When they asked how much we expected to raise, Jack and I thought $300 seemed reasonable. After all, this was a fundraiser with a bunch of broke college students. So we drew the thermometer with $25 increments, inching toward bubble letters that read "$300 Goal" at the top. I wasn't positive we could raise that much money, but at least this would be a fun way to let friends know what Jack and I had planned after graduation.

My five roommates and I made our way to the liquor store on M Street and pooled our rewards points to rent a keg. We posted on Facebook and invited everyone we knew, leaving people wondering if this was an elaborate prank or a real campaign. My roommate Brian shared the announcement video, along with the caption: "Please help me get rid of my roommate Will. I've been trying to get away from him for two years to no avail. If he wins CT State Senate, he'll have to move back home. . . ."

When the party started and people made their way upstairs to donate, we used a red marker to color in the thermometer. To our surprise, we exceeded the $300 goal in the first half hour. By the end of the party, we'd raised over $8,000. When I went to bed that night, my head was spinning—and I never touched the keg.

I can hardly describe how moved I was that so many of my classmates were willing to donate to a random, down-ballot race in Connecticut. Conventional wisdom and punditry had convinced me that much of my generation was apathetic about politics, so it came as no surprise when a chicken sandwich won the write-in vote to be our class president. But instead of rolling their eyes and asking why anybody would want to run for office, students shuffled into the party and asked about my climate change platform and gun violence prevention plans. Perhaps our generation was apathetic in the eyes of politicians who embodied a bygone era, but clearly young people were responding positively to the idea of someone their age being on the ballot. We had stumbled upon a generational excitement, or perhaps exasperation, about who gets a seat at the table where decisions are made. That dorm-room fundraiser tapped into the enthusiasm of young people—something that would prove to be a game changer once we hit the ground in Connecticut.

8

You Can Never Wear Shorts Again

Halfway toward our fundraising goal, I started to get calls from professional campaign operatives. Connecticut is a small state, and its political arena is even smaller. Each campaign cycle, a small cadre of people juggle dozens of campaigns across the state. They work hard, aren't particularly attached to any candidate, and make quite a bit of money. After all, thanks to the Citizens' Election Program, every campaign for the Connecticut State Senate has a budget of over $100,000.

Throughout the semester, I fielded a handful of calls from these campaign gurus who bragged about all of the experience they had. Listening politely as I stocked the shelves at Snaxa, it occurred to me that they probably didn't know I had already hired Jack and Maryli. Nevertheless, I was happy to listen to their free advice.

Oddly enough, they all exuded confidence that our campaign would win. That raised some alarm bells, because even I thought winning was only possible, not probable. Maryli wouldn't even go that far. Eventually, I came to understand that their confidence was feigned. They didn't actually care if I won or if I lost. After all, I had a lot more at stake in this election than they did. While political consultants collect a paycheck regardless of the outcome, candidates are unemployed if the campaign goes south. I didn't know much about building a team, but I knew that I wanted to work with people who told me the truth.

One day, someone put me in touch with Isaac and Emily from BerlinRosen. BerlinRosen is a Democratic consulting firm based in New York, and their services aren't cheap. Hiring them would take up a significant portion of our budget, but they came highly recommended and had a reputation for running sleek, modern campaigns.

To my surprise, Isaac and Emily offered to come all the way down to DC to talk about our campaign. As my friends flew across the country for job interviews, it felt bizarre that anyone would board a flight or train to meet with me and Jack. Where would we even sit down together? We could bring them to our dorm, but there was always a chance that one of my roommates would be sitting on the couch in boxers playing video games. We considered renting out a classroom, but that felt too much like a school project.

Thankfully, BerlinRosen had a small office downtown. When Jack and I arrived, they handed us a big stack of flyers and brochures from past campaigns, and I felt a sinking disappointment. These guys were supposed to be the best at what they do—did they really think sending flyers through the mail was going to win an election? Personally, I had checked my mailbox frequently while waiting for college decisions, and maybe twice since then. Surely a twenty-first-century campaign required replacing stale tactics like this one.

Isaac sensed my skepticism and began explaining that I wasn't the target demographic. Statistically speaking, someone my age wasn't likely to vote in a midterm election.

"Listen, you've got a slight chance of winning this thing," he said, with a realism that was refreshing. "But only if you win over older voters." Seniors check their mail religiously, Emily explained, and many actually rely on flyers to help decide which candidate will earn their vote.

Yes, Isaac conceded, most voters take only a passing glance at the brochures and leaflets before tossing them in the garbage. That rang true, as I had spent much of my childhood sorting through the trash trying to find report cards, permission slips, or college decisions my mom had thrown away. She tossed anything that even slightly resembled junk mail.

"But those fleeting moments before the flyer reaches the garbage are where the election is won and lost," Emily told us. Both Emily and Isaac had done their research. They ran through the changing demographics of the Twenty-Sixth District and recent voting history. The district had narrowly voted for Romney, then flipped heavily for Clinton in 2016.

For about an hour, they explained to Jack and me the difference between persuasion targeting (reaching out to people who will definitely vote but might support either the Democrat or the Republican) and mobilization targeting (reaching out to steadfast Democrats who might forget to vote in midterm elections). Along the way, they name-dropped some of the major clients they had helped win.

Then the conversation shifted to my age. Unlike every other campaign consultant who had called my cell phone over the last few weeks, Isaac and Emily weren't shy about the downside of running for office at twenty-two. Many voters have a visceral opposition to voting for someone who is younger than their kids or even their grandkids.

"That's why we use permission theory," Emily said.

"Instead of putting Will on every mailer, we'll feature parents and grandparents, maybe a lifelong Republican who isn't voting for Boucher anymore," Isaac jumped in.

"You're not going to put Will on the mailers?" Jack asked.

"We'll put him on some of them. But we'll also put older people talking *about* Will. We need to give voters permission to jump ship even if they used to vote for Boucher," Emily went on.

"Look, there's a group of people who are going to see Will's face, maybe pinch his cheeks, but wouldn't dream of voting for him,"

Isaac said. "Those folks need to read about Will, but they don't need to see him."

Their advice was honest. When the meeting ended, Isaac added one last suggestion.

"I know you're in college right now, but you really can never wear shorts," he said. I looked down at my outfit and laughed, but he wasn't kidding. "You need to look older than you are, so you can't afford to let anyone confuse you for the paperboy. Pants only."

Jack and I rented scooters and made our way back to campus, reflecting on the meeting as we wove through tourists on the National Mall. Jack rightfully pointed out that Isaac and Emily were expensive, and their advice was a little harsh. But I was already sold, because we could count on them to tell us the truth.

9

Building a Campaign and a Bunk Bed

The campaign was launched, our fundraising was off to a good start, and a team was in place. The only problem? I was almost 300 miles away from the district I was hoping to represent. And it was becoming increasingly clear that campaigning by phone had its limitations.

So, while our friends packed their bags for a wild spring break on the beaches of Florida, Jack and I planned a wild week in Connecticut. We lined up fundraisers nearly every day to help us reach the $15,000 threshold. Local Democrats who believed in my campaign (or were too nice to say no) hosted small coffees, as did the parents of some friends from high school and even my dentist. We stuffed our vacation to the max, racing between two, three, or four fundraisers each day. It was exhausting but exhilarating, and I felt like momentum was building. I'd never done much public speaking, but delivering a "stump speech" multiple times a day gave me an opportunity to get better at each event. I learned where to pause, how to read the room, and when to skip to the end if guests seemed restless. In the car ride between events, Jack would give his notes:

"Stop telling that joke, it's not as funny as you think it is."

"You mispronounced the host's name."

"Strong ending that time, but you forgot to ask for money."

One night, I learned that Ned Lamont had organized a fundraiser nearby. Lamont, a Democrat who had previously run for the U.S. Senate, was now running for governor. This was my only night with a clear schedule, and Jack was looking forward to eating something other than a cheese plate for dinner. But I'd never met a gubernatorial candidate before, so I decided to spend the evening at someone else's fundraiser.

When Lamont walked into the living room, he had no security guard, nor any aura of grandeur. His daughter was checking people in at the door, making his campaign seem as humble as ours. Unlike the stereotypical politician, Lamont seemed hesitant to interrupt anyone's conversation as he walked around the room. He scarfed down appetizers with an eagerness that made him look more like a party crasher than the guest of honor.

I walked over to introduce myself and let him know that I was running for the state Senate. Lamont chuckled, appearing to get a kick out of the idea of a college student running for office. We shook hands, and I don't think either of us thought the other would win.

Lamont's speech, much like the man I'd eventually get to know, was conversational and nonchalant. He didn't attack the other Democrats vying for the nomination, nor the Republicans running for governor. Instead, he focused on Connecticut's future. From the back of the crowd, a middle-aged man asked what Lamont would have done to prevent General Electric from leaving Connecticut.

It sounds like a simple question, but it's a fraught issue in Fairfield County. For many voters in my community, GE's 2016 departure from their corporate headquarters in Fairfield, Connecticut, amounted to a seismic shift in our state's prospects. The company had been a central part of our regional identity, as thousands of employees had bought homes and raised their families in the nearby suburbs. Corporations like GE, nestled in bucolic office parks, had contributed greatly to the explosion of wealth along Connecticut's Gold Coast. For middle- and upper-income residents, the company's decision to leave effectively confirmed their suspicions that taxes were untenably high and this state was mismanaged.

In reality, GE had been showered in corporate tax favors by policy-makers who were desperate for them to stay. All the while, our state could barely afford to hand out any tax breaks at all. Pension obligations were coming due, working families needed more support than ever to recover from the Great Recession of 2007–2009, and state leaders had decided to start paying our bills proactively rather than burden the next generation with debt. Admittedly, Connecticut was no longer a tax haven.

But GE didn't leave for Florida, Texas, New Hampshire, or some other state without an income tax. They went to Massachusetts, where both corporations and their high-earning executives pay more to the state government than they do in Connecticut. This left some politicians to posit that GE left because Connecticut's governor hadn't treated GE's C-suite with the respect they "deserved." Others, more plausibly, suspected that executives had grown tired of schlepping all the way to New York's airports. It's true that Fairfield County, a wealthy community, rather uniquely lacks convenient access to a major air terminal.

But the most honest answer came from company leaders themselves; they were leaving Connecticut in search of a "diverse, technologically fluent workforce"—something Massachusetts was better able to provide. GE's CFO noted that "young talent today want to be in a vibrant, open, interactive, high-tech, fun kind of space." He called Fairfield County a "morgue."

At first glance, the notion of a weak workforce pipeline in Connecticut seemed preposterous. Although Connecticut's schools are vastly unequal, many of our public school districts were considered the best in the country. Plus, there was no shortage of first-rate institutions of higher education in Connecticut. From Yale to Wesleyan to the University of Connecticut, about 150,000 college students are pursuing a degree here during any given year.

But while many Harvard and MIT grads launch their careers in Massachusetts after earning their degree, most Yale or Wesleyan students flee Connecticut once graduation ceremonies come to a close. GE executives were right that young people want to start their careers in vibrant metropolises, and they won't find a Connecticut city with more than 150,000 people. Sadly, the small cities we do have are suffering from decades of neglect. As suburbs amassed wealth, they built tall hedges and local governance structures to shield them from poverty, gun violence, and a responsibility to help their less-affluent neighbors. Sometime during the era when corporate office parks were in vogue, towns like Westport, Wilton, and New Canaan seemed to forget that the vitality of our economy relied on the success of nearby cities like Bridgeport, Norwalk, and Stamford. The suburbs are unaffordable to recent graduates, and the cities aren't exactly bustling. Young people are drawn to public transportation, but Connecticut's aging infrastructure offers only a bumper-to-bumper commute each day. Even the stream of young parents moving out to the suburbs slowed, as New York became increasingly safe and family friendly.

As a result, our state finds itself with the sixth-oldest workforce in the country: one in four workers are over the age of fifty-five. Some of the millennials who work in Fairfield County are so desperate to live elsewhere that they endure a reverse commute every day. A quarter mile from Katie's house sits the headquarters of Bridgewater, the wealthiest hedge fund in the world. Although its campus is shrouded by tall trees and secrecy, it's impossible not to notice the daily parade of large, black buses that carry young employees between the office and their apartments in Manhattan. Why rely on this company-chartered bus? Because Connecticut's trains have slowed to an untenable pace, and the only way to compete for top talent is to pay for private transportation. In short, diagnosing Connecticut's economic difficulties is challenging not because it's hard to find the problem, but because it's hard to know where to start.

Nevertheless, GE's departure poured gasoline on the embers of resentment regarding declining real estate values and unpopular income tax rates. As the C-suite packed their boxes (or, more likely, paid someone else to pack their boxes), they turned the page on an era of leafy corporate office parks and grassy suburban sprawl.

"Connecticut's economic future relies on more young people calling this state home," Lamont said. He glanced around the room, looking unsure if his answer had swayed a room full of business types who might have preferred a promise to cut taxes. "We need more young people like Will Haskell," he said. People started looking around, wondering who Will Haskell was.

I was shocked that Lamont even remembered my name, let alone included me in his remarks. On the drive home, I started to think about how Connecticut's story intersected with my own. I'd gotten the GE question at my own fundraisers, and I had ticked off talking points about revitalizing a dormant airport in Bridgeport, cutting traffic on I-95, and investing in the high-quality public schools that draw young families to Connecticut. But Lamont's casual aside made me realize that I could speak more personally about my decision to come home. For one thing, nearly everyone I'd gone to high school with was planning to live in Boston, New York, San Francisco, or Los Angeles. I realized that while I lacked the experience, perspective, or authority to talk fluently about thorny questions of policy, I could speak with some insight about how to make Connecticut enticing to the next generation.

To start with, I was learning firsthand just how hard it is to afford an apartment in Fairfield County. In addition to raising campaign funds, Jack and I had another project to tackle over spring break: finding a place to live. With the help of a slightly annoyed local realtor who typically caters to a higher tax bracket, we eventually found an apartment we could afford in New Canaan. The apartment was really just the second floor of a vacant nail salon, and the thermostat for the building was locked away somewhere on the first floor. Although questions about amenities would go unanswered, we occasionally bothered the landlord as he worked at the hair salon next door. We knew he was in if his bright-green Lamborghini was parked outside. He taught karate in the garage, meaning the driveway was sporadically filled with children and consequently unavailable. Also, the rent was paid to his ex-wife. The situation was . . . odd.

The apartment consisted of a kitchen, a bedroom, and an oddly large bathroom that doubled as our walk-in closet. Rent was $1,000, which Jack and I split fifty-fifty. Although New Canaan's downtown wasn't exactly bustling, we were relieved to see that Tequila Mockingbird, around the corner, stayed open to the wee hours of 10 p.m.

After signing the lease, Jack and I drove to IKEA and loaded his Mazda with one bunk bed, two mattresses, a half dozen dishes, and a dozen cinnamon buns. With a few hours to kill before the next fundraiser, we got to work on building the bunk bed—a task that made building a campaign look easy. I misread the instructions, and we had to start over at least twice. When we were finally done, I noticed three screws were left over. Jack asked which bed I wanted, and I was sure to grab the top bunk.

By the time spring break ended, we had raised the $15,000 we needed to qualify for public financing. When it came to bank accounts, we were now on equal footing with our opponent, and I could begin asking for votes instead of checks. Perhaps most importantly, the speed with which we had raised our qualifying funds sent a signal to skeptical Democrats that I was serious about this campaign. Of course, there were thousands of people we'd yet to convince. After all, Boucher was a popular incumbent who had built relationships with seemingly everyone around town. Even those who came to our fundraisers would sometimes approach Jack before leaving and ask that we not include them in any photographs from the event. "I can't offend my friend Toni," they explained.

10

Don't Tell Me to Call My Legislators. Help Me Replace Them.

Everyone loves to remind second-semester seniors to savor their final moments of college. "Being an adult sucks," reported one friend who had recently graduated. "So don't forget to enjoy every minute before graduating." My mom, nostalgic for her college years, gloomily commented on my Instagram that I'd "never have this much fun again!" But while I was trying to make the most out of friendships and courses, I was constantly distracted by calls, texts, and emails from the Twenty-Sixth District. I started to feel like I was leading a double life, stepping away from a college party to take a call about Connecticut's pension liabilities.

On one rainy night in March, my a cappella group was making its way to Catholic University in DC, all of us jammed into the back of an Uber. This was an annual gig that didn't pay but ended with a party for other a cappella groups in the DC area. It was exactly as dorky as it sounds, and we loved it.

But this year, I had commitments in Connecticut the next morning. March for Our Lives rallies were popping up across the country in reaction to a tragic shooting at Marjory Stoneman Douglas High School in Parkland, Florida, and I was invited to speak at events in Hartford and Westport.

I'd been so busy enjoying college that I hadn't yet written a speech. From the back of the Uber, I jotted down some thoughts on my phone. I'd been asked to say something about my generation's perspective on gun violence, but I'd never spoken at a rally before. Just weeks earlier, David Hogg and Emma Gonzalez, survivors of the Parkland shooting, had looked straight into a CNN camera and spoken from the heart about a political system that prioritizes campaign contributions from the NRA over the lives of children. Connecticut, too, had been shaken by gun violence, not just at Sandy Hook Elementary School but also in regular shootings that the papers barely covered. The previous year, Bridgeport saw twenty-three homicides, although most people in the nearby suburbs hadn't heard about them.

I wanted to talk about the numbness to tragedy that had become commonplace in my generation, and convey that repeated tragedies had forced us to mature sooner than we should have. I wanted to offer hope that our generation might eventually forge a new political dynamic that wasn't bought and sold by special interests.

At the party after the concert, I thought about what I'd say as I made my way through that cloud of sweat and stale beer that makes every college basement smell the same. Red cups, overflowing with some bright-pink concoction, were passed around. My friends were mixing and mingling, but I started to feel out of place. The two worlds I was trying to straddle now seemed irreconcilable. In just a few hours, I'd board an Amtrak and speak alongside family members who had lost their loved ones to gun violence. But at the moment, "Shake It Off" was playing so loudly that nobody could hear their own thoughts. Could politicians still have fun? Were state senators supposed to act like state senators all the time? Following politics had taught me that elected officials were either robots who didn't enjoy human pleasures or so deeply human that their vices precipitated their downfall. Maybe young people didn't run for office because it precluded them from living a normal life. Did David Hogg and Emma Gonzalez still have fun with their friends when they weren't on TV?

I couldn't shake the feeling that I had done something wrong by trying to be both a college student and a candidate, so I went back to campus to get some sleep before my early morning trip home.

When I arrived at Connecticut's capitol the next day, I promised myself that I wouldn't let the scale of the building freak me out again. Last time I visited, I was just toying with the idea of running for office. Now I was a declared candidate.

This time it wasn't the scale of the building that threw me off, but the size of the crowd. I had imagined a small gathering of students, and I was prepared to speak casually about our shared desire for change. I had a few statistics memorized, and a quote that Katie had texted me by Justice Louis Brandeis about states being a laboratory of democracy.

But when I saw the thousands of protesters gathered in Bushnell Park, I realized I'd better write something down. I sat in my car and scribbled down the statistics, and the quote. Loud chants started echoing from Bushnell Park, and I worried that my speech sounded too much like a research paper and not enough like a call to action. So I jotted down some closing lines that felt more urgent: "Don't tell me to pray. Instead, help me to act. Don't tell me to call my legislators. Instead, help me replace them."

The park was filled with thousands of people, not marching so much as walking around and holding signs. I wondered whether that Instagram message I'd received was truly an invitation to speak or just an invitation to attend the rally. Maybe all of these people had also received a message on Instagram. I awkwardly introduced myself to a handful of activists and complimented people on their signs, T-shirts, and buttons. I didn't yet have a politician's skill at striking up a conversation with strangers.

Suddenly, a University of Bridgeport student named Tyler grabbed my arm and hung a "SPEAKER" badge around my neck. He was in a rush, but he handed me the agenda for the rally and told me not to venture too far from the stage. To my surprise, the agenda said that Tyler would open the rally and then introduce . . . me. Further down the list, I saw members of Congress and state legislators who had actually won elections and passed laws. My toes started to clench.

As the music quieted down and eyes turned toward the stage, Tyler nudged my arm and said he was amazed to see someone from our generation running for office. He pulled me up front and introduced me to the other folks who would be speaking, including politicians who seemed perturbed that I had somehow secured a speaking slot ahead of them. Suddenly, a familiar voice called out my name. Jonathan was making his way up to the stage when a student activist stopped him and asked for his badge.

"That's my state representative," I told the organizer, and Jonathan seemed more than a little surprised that I had any clout around here. That made two of us.

It was only once I reached the podium that I could see just how many thousands of people were gathered in the park. When it was my turn to speak, the echo from the speaker made it nearly impossible to hear myself.

". . . So let's launch an experiment here in Connecticut not just in democracy but in compassion, in empathy, in resolve, and in courage. Let's show the rest of the world that what we do here can be done everywhere. Please don't tell me to pray; instead, help me to act. Don't tell me to call my legislators; instead, help me replace them. And don't tell me to wait, because the time for reform was yesterday."

At the end of my speech, I realized I had been shouting.

The response from the crowd was electrifying. When I stepped back, one of the congressmen elbowed my side and told me that Boucher must be getting nervous. On the drive home, a small part of me assumed that running for office meant speaking at rallies like this a lot. Once our campaign got underway, I learned that getting thirty people to a meet and greet was a resounding victory and a big crowd.

I made it back to Westport just in time for the next rally. This group was much smaller, but there were still a few hundred people gathered on Main Street. In fact, this crowd made me more nervous because it was filled with the people I had grown up alongside. When I stepped up to the microphone, I saw Boucher standing right beside me. I'd never actually seen her in person, and I didn't expect that she would be here today. She was wearing the same red pantsuit that she wore to the gubernatorial debate I had watched over YouTube. Boucher is short, with jet-black hair that she keeps in a neat bob. Her face is expressive as others are talking, and she's generous with a laugh or a round of applause when the speaker is clearly expecting one. She seemed to greet every person at the rally with a smile or a wave, making it hard to tell who she truly knew and who she didn't. After two decades of practice, she had retail politics down to a T. From far away, I'd slipped into thinking of Boucher as a villain. Up close, she looked more like a friendly neighbor who just happened to be a Republican.

Surely I couldn't deliver the same speech, with the final line calling to replace her. I decided to soften the last line, ending the speech with, "Don't tell me to pray. Instead, help me to act."

Once the rally was over, I turned to my state senator and introduced myself. She told me how impressed she was that I was running, then quickly moved on and began shaking other hands. When I got back to Georgetown, I told Jack the good news: thousands of young people were ready for change in Connecticut, and Boucher wasn't taking our campaign seriously.

11

Coming Home

When the sun rises over Washington, DC, the Lincoln Memorial's marble turns from a sterile white into a glowing gold. I'd spent the last four years living as a student in DC, bringing every visiting friend and family member to see the monument and compare it with a five-dollar bill. But the tourists were gone at this hour, and the steps leading to Lincoln's neoclassical temple were decorated with hungover students. By tradition, Georgetown seniors celebrate their final night of college by staying up late and gathering together to watch the sunrise over the National Mall. My classmates all felt some mix of excitement and dread about the jobs they were about to begin, the cities they were about to explore, the lives they were about to launch.

My mind was filled with a million questions. Was this my last night of fun for the foreseeable future? Everyone else spoke with such confidence about the paths they had chosen—had I made a huge mistake? Most pressingly, the nominating convention was in forty-eight hours. What was I going to say?

Eventually, we meandered back to campus, not particularly thrilled about the prospect of putting on black gowns and sitting in a hot auditorium. When we reached our dorm, a few of my roommates took advantage of the free hour to sleep. I loaded my clothes into big garbage bags, just as I had done four years ago when I left Connecticut and arrived on campus. As I packed, I thought about what life would look like when "Pomp and Circumstance" stopped playing.

My friends were moving to exciting cities, launching lucrative careers, enrolling in grad school, or surrounding themselves with the people they loved. Was I about to seriously screw up my twenties?

When I was growing up, my mom venerated that decade of her life. Having graduated from an all-women's college, she moved to Boston for law school and spent those years barhopping with friends and dating guys who weren't my dad. She'd sometimes take me to Boston and track down her old apartments as though we were walking the Freedom Trail. When I eventually put on my cap and smiled at my family in the bleachers, I was a ball of sweat and stress underneath, worrying about what I'd gotten myself into.

The next morning, Jack and I piled back into his Mazda, and our friends Liam and Emily tagged along for a ride up the Eastern Seaboard. Between the four of us, there was so much luggage that Jack couldn't see anything out the back window. A consummate rule follower, this kind of driving violation would normally be a nonstarter for him. But there were too many other things to be stressed about today, and he barely registered the rear-window issue.

Later that night, the Democratic and Republican parties of Connecticut would hold nominating conventions to select their candidates for the state Senate. In many Senate districts, this is when a race is won or lost. In overwhelmingly liberal districts, for example, a candidate just needs to win the Democratic nomination in order to win the seat. In some cities, the convention is a boisterous evening filled with competing speeches and party bosses whipping delegate votes.

Conventions in the Twenty-Sixth District are much sleepier. The Republicans found two prominent officials to nominate Boucher, and her speech brimmed with confidence that seemed to say she planned to continue serving this district until she either retired or was elected governor. In a normal year, the Democrats would nominate a party loyalist who had been convinced to run without much expectation of winning.

Jack and I wanted to organize a different sort of convention. We hoped to send a signal from the very start that we were running to win. Perhaps most importantly, we wanted to invite people who weren't party insiders to join our team. I'd spent the last few weeks calling each of the delegates, learning where their children and grandchildren went to college, listening to their stories about past campaigns, and politely understanding their skepticism about my candidacy. I'd gently remind them that no other Democrat was running, and I asked for their support at the convention. Some agreed enthusiastically, others begrudgingly.

As we made our way up I-95, Emily and Liam slept in the back seat while Jack and I worked on my convention speech. We had learned at the fundraisers that vague attacks on Boucher weren't landing, and we needed to be specific in criticizing her voting record. As Jack saw it, an implausible candidate became more plausible through specificity, so we focused on concrete failures of public policy. We jammed as many numbers into the speech as possible.

Somewhere between Wilmington and Philadelphia, we typed out, "We've settled into a routine in Connecticut that's just not working. Our politics are broken, and our community is suffering as a result. More than 350 of our bridges are crumbling from decades of neglect. Those who commute from Westport to Grand Central spend 29 whole days—almost a month of their life—each year on a train that's actually gotten slower since 1950. A ten-minute drive on I-95 will take you across a $100,000 difference in median income. Huge disparities in income aren't just morally wrong—they're also bad for the economy. The opioid epidemic has caused drug overdoses in Connecticut to reach historic highs, taking over 1,000 lives last year. We're facing budget deficits of $1.9 billion in fiscal year 2020, $2.7 billion in 2021, and $3.2 billion in 2022. Connecticut may be a great state, but we've been taken down the wrong path by policy makers who've grown too comfortable in their seats."

Once we reached Connecticut, we picked up 150 lawn signs that had been delivered to my mom's garage, then made our way to our apartment in New Canaan. Liam hung the thermometer poster from our dorm-room fundraiser above the couch while Emily tried to figure out how to break into the salon downstairs and turn on the A/C. Jack sat on the bunk bed and put finishing touches on the speech while I showered, shaved, and put on a suit. I lingered in the shower, a bit spooked by having seen our lawn signs up close for the first time. Were we really going to find anyone who wanted to put a sign with my name in their front yard? It was also dawning on me just how lonely this endeavor would be for Jack and me. In college, we were surrounded by people even when we didn't want to be. With Liam and Emily leaving tomorrow morning, we wouldn't have anyone to join us at Tequila Mockingbird.

Back in Jack's Mazda, we hopped on the Merritt Parkway and headed to the convention. I pointed out to Emily and Liam that the Merritt is often so filled with traffic, no one bothers to look at the art deco bridges and lush greenery surrounding the parkway. When I was little, my dad used to point out the intricacies of each bridge and explain how they reflected the character of that particular town. It was a story of government at its best, as the state and federal government had worked together to hire out-of-work artists and tradesmen to build the parkway during the Great Depression. At the groundbreaking of the Merritt Parkway, Congressman Merritt noted that "this great highway is not being constructed primarily for rapid transit but for pleasant transit." These days, grinding traffic turns the Merritt into a parking lot every morning and afternoon. You'd be hard-pressed to find a commuter who describes their daily experience as either rapid or pleasant.

We got off the parkway at Exit 42 and navigated a death-defying intersection where I'd nearly totaled my car the first time I picked up

Katie for a date. We passed Coffee An', a donut shop where signed portraits of politicians are ignored by customers hoping to snag a homemade donut before they sell out at noon. I pointed across the Saugatuck River at my grandparents' house, where I spent afternoons and evenings while my mom worked late.

I told them about my grandfather, who we call Big Bob, and how he sat with me in that house to work through my math homework every week. Around the age of sixty, Big Bob had left his job as a chemical engineer and started teaching math and science in one of the Bronx's most under-resourced high schools. Students threatened him with knives and threw textbooks at his head, but Big Bob was the right combination of tough and compassionate for the job. He built relationships with the students and stayed up late at night trying to figure out how to make his lessons more engaging. When commuting to and from the Bronx became too challenging, Big Bob became a substitute teacher in the Westport schools. Every once in a while, I would walk into band practice to find him waving the baton, or into French class to find him wearing a beret. When the teacher returned the next day, usually furious that the substitute hadn't followed his or her lesson plan, I didn't disclose that my grandfather was the man who had opted to share life lessons instead.

As we drove by their house, I could predict with near certainty that my grandmother, who I call Meem, was inside either working through the *New York Times* daily crossword puzzle or wringing her hands that I was too skinny. Meem and I spent so much time together when I was little that I actually started to call her "Mom." She devised a quick course correction and has been Meem ever since. In my rotating after-school schedule, she was the only person ever to arrive on time when school was dismissed. She even started driving my friends home, developing an encyclopedic knowledge of Greens Farms Elementary School's class of 2007.

We crossed the Saugatuck River on the Ruth Steinkraus Cohen Bridge, where I'd seen protesters gather for years to criticize the war in Iraq. Westport has a history of activism, though it can hardly be considered a progressive paradise. Martin Luther King Jr. had once spoken at a synagogue in town, but less than five percent of my graduating class was Black. My hometown was considered racially progressive among Fairfield County suburbs for allowing students from the nearby city of Bridgeport to fill empty seats in the public schools. MSNBC may not have been playing in most households, but neither was Fox. CNN and CNBC were more popular, although no substantive news station could hold a candle to the audience of *Westport Now*, a local blog that contained mostly photos of sunrises at the beach and local arrest reports.

Most of the families I grew up around found it impolite to talk about politics over dinner, and when public policy came up, it was always weighed through an unmistakably suburban lens. Conversations about immigration, even among those who were inclined to support greater access to citizenship, came back to "my housekeeper" or "my gardener." Those who loved *An Inconvenient Truth* bought Priuses that lined the Post Road, but also installed irrigation systems to keep their sprawling lawns green. Ninety-six percent of my high school class went on to four-year institutions, although many could probably have gotten a great education at one of Connecticut's community colleges. Local zoning authorities had spent decades blocking the development of apartment buildings, which explained why I rarely had a teacher in the Westport public schools who could actually afford to live in town.

Despite all this, I wanted to believe that my hometown had a liberal heart, or could get there with some prodding. After crossing the bridge, we passed the Gillespie Center, one of the only homeless shelters located in the suburbs of Fairfield County. The town of Westport had supported John Kerry, Barack Obama twice, and most recently, Hillary Clinton by a two-to-one margin. Even the Republican first selectman was a vocal supporter of gun regulations.

Not quite ready to arrive at the convention, I asked Jack to stop by Burying Hill Beach. Liam took out a deck of cards, and we played poker on a picnic table for a few minutes in near silence. I tried to process that college was over and a new chapter had started. But it felt strange to launch adulthood in the same town where I had grown up—the small town I thought I had outgrown. Driving around brought back a flood of memories from being a kid in Westport, but it also reminded me of how little I had in common with the adults here. What did I know about the daily lives of the voters who lived in these McMansions?

The "Westporters" my age were graduating from college this month and heading to New York. Winning over this town entailed more than just reconnecting with old friends; it would require winning over their parents. Jack and I were about to launch a campaign centered on paid family leave, gun violence prevention, and economic inequality. In order to succeed in November, we'd need to figure out how to frame these issues in a way that resonated with those who were on the winning side of that inequity. A young Democratic socialist named Alexandria Ocasio-Cortez was winning over the Bronx and Queens block by block, unapologetically championing Medicare for all. We were tepidly peering down long driveways and hoping that everyone could at least agree that prescription drugs were too expensive.

Jack had taken a big leap of faith, moving to Fairfield County practically sight unseen. Now I felt a sense of responsibility about his life outside of work. Would he make friends? Where, other than McDonalds, could we get a cheap meal? As if Jack could sense my worries, he helpfully steered me to focus on the present and rehearse the speech one last time. Then it was time to head over to town hall.

Katie arrived at the same time, driving a car filled with blue balloons. I stuffed six breath mints in my mouth while Jack set up a few lawn signs out front. When we discovered that the auditorium was already half full with family, friends, and strangers, I swallowed most of the mints. As the delegates arrived, some of them seemed to wonder if they had the wrong room, given the lively atmosphere and growing crowd. I introduced myself to those I had only met over the phone and spent extra time talking to those who seemed annoyed to be there.

I had asked Jonathan, Westport's own representative, to nominate me. Jonathan had come to see this race as winnable, and I had come to see him as a friend. To second Jonathan's nomination, I asked Rudy Marconi, Ridgefield's first selectman. Rudy had served as Ridgefield's chief executive for more than two decades, and he was beloved in town. His was the second-largest town in the Twenty-Sixth District, but I didn't know anyone there. Rudy was kind enough to take me out for a cup of coffee before I graduated and encouraged me to run. Eventually I'd learn that first selectmen rely on having a good relationship with their legislative delegation, regardless of political party. Those relationships can make a crucial difference to securing funding for schools, roads, or other town priorities. Rudy had a lot to lose by supporting my campaign, and he took a big risk by enthusiastically agreeing to second my nomination.

Jonathan's and Rudy's speeches lent credibility to my candidacy by speaking directly to Democrats who were still on the fence. "Every once in a while, you run into somebody you might call an old soul," Jonathan told the crowd. "I need Will Haskell in Hartford. As a collaborator, as a partner, and as a friend."

I also asked Big Bob to "third" my nomination. He is famously bad at memorizing anything, and you can always spot him in the back of his church choir, eyes glued to the music as though it's his first time singing the hymn. When he got to the podium, he read a few thoughts he'd prepared about my appetite for chicken nuggets and strawberry ice cream. But when he started to talk about my mom, and how much I'd learned from her work ethic, he looked up and seemed to forget his notes. The delegates loved his speech, so much so that one delegate approached me to ask if he was single.

Katie squeezed my hand to say it was time to leave, and we were almost out the door when Melissa from the Westport DTC flagged me down.

"Don't forget the most important part!" she said.

"What's that?"

"You need to sign this form to get your name on the ballot."

I borrowed her pen, and just like that, I was the Democratic candidate for the Connecticut State Senate in the Twenty-Sixth District. The first major hurdle was over. Now we just had to win in November.

12

Knock, Knock

"**M**y boss chews so loudly."

"She ran out of work to give me."

"Mine hasn't let me go home before midnight once this week."

After you graduate from college, the group texts that used to be filled with people looking for company in the dining hall become filled with complaints about everyone's first boss. Jack and I couldn't relate, since we were the ones who decided when to wake up, how late to work, and how to direct our efforts. We may not have been focused on making a good impression on any one supervisor, but we were obsessed with making hundreds of good impressions every single day. As we saw it, every voter was a potential boss. In order to get this job, I had to wake up and nail a few dozen interviews a day, whether at front doors, community events, or meet and greets.

Luckily, I needn't have worried about Jack settling into suburbia. He adjusted to New Canaan with ease, signing up for a library membership, developing a preference for Trader Joe's over Stop & Shop, and cooking dinner most nights. Even in college, Jack had the schedule of a middle-aged dad, waking up hours before anyone else on campus and often falling asleep upstairs before the party downstairs had ended.

My schedule was less conventional, then and now. I woke up late, spent a few hours studying for the LSAT, and then started knocking on doors. As anyone who has worked on a campaign will tell you, "canvasing" is a sweaty and exhausting endeavor. Keep in mind, these seven towns are famous for their expansive lawns, and infamous for their four-acre exclusionary zoning. It could take fifteen minutes to walk from one house to the next. The hottest or rainiest afternoons were miserable, but Katie's grandmother had taught me that those were the days when you'd find the most people at home.

I actually came to enjoy knocking on doors each afternoon. Since my days were otherwise filled with small talk and stump speeches, I appreciated the quiet time. It was almost therapeutic to gather my thoughts as I trotted down each driveway, thinking through how I'd introduce myself at the next door. When a conversation didn't go as planned, I had a few minutes to wonder what in the world I was doing here, and to remind myself why I wanted this job anyway.

Along the way, I got to know the communities I was hoping to represent. Although I knew just about every street in Westport, I'd only been to Wilton, Ridgefield, and Bethel a handful of times. In fact, one of the hardest questions I got from a local reporter was where I liked to eat in Wilton. I'd prepared for a hundred policy topics, but that question stumped me. When I went out to knock on doors, I learned that cell service cut out in the northern part of New Canaan, traffic built up around Belden Hill Road in Wilton on Sundays when the Congregational Church let out, and Weston's Lunch Box made a mean chicken parm sandwich.

Whenever campaigning brought me through Westport, I'd stop at my grandparents' so that Big Bob could shake his head and ask why I was bothering folks at their front door. Katie agreed, and she liked to remind me that she hides upstairs when a stranger rings her doorbell. If voters came to the door at only one of every three houses, what was the point?

Initially, my answer was, "This is what everyone else does." But soon I had a better one. Sure, there were plenty of people who hit the floor when I rang the bell. And when they did open the door, I'd sometimes make a terrible impression. There was the time I was greeted by a voter who came to the door in the nude, or the time I narrowly escaped injury from a mean-looking dog and his irate owner. One afternoon I accidentally stumbled into a shiva, although they welcomed me inside for a brief and awkward conversation. But after 4,000 doors, I saw the value in this tried-and-true method of campaigning. And I got better along the way.

First, I learned not to rush into my stump speech.

"Hello, [INSERT NAME HERE], my name is Will Haskell and I'm running to be your state senator. I believe in stronger gun laws and transportation investme—"

At that point, the voter usually faked a phone call or politely took my flyer and promised to read up on the campaign. It took me about 1,000 doors to figure out that their reaction wasn't a rejection of my platform, but instead an aversion to being lectured. In the eyes of these potential voters, I was another telemarketer selling them a magazine subscription or a missionary offering a shot at eternal life. In fact, so many voters thought I was there to deliver a free copy of *The Book of Mormon* that I retired my black tie for a while.

Eventually, I learned to treat every door as a chance to learn about the people I was hoping to represent. No one would remember my plan to fund faster trains, but they might remember a conversation about the topic that mattered most to them.

I started to ask every voter the same question: What's the most important issue to you? Most of the time, I had little to contribute to the problem they mentioned. Lots of people brought up President Trump, but just as many brought up trash collection or the timeliness of their child's school bus. I listened to people vent about the federal, state, and municipal government, and in doing so I learned about their lives. I heard from commuters that the cell reception along the ride to Manhattan was spotty at best, so I made internet connectivity a part of my transportation platform. One gentleman in Wilton brought me to the end of his driveway to show me what he believed to be the largest pothole in the state of Connecticut.

Listening to voters didn't just make me a better candidate. Eventually it made me a better state senator. Months later, I'd help launch a partnership with AT&T to provide high-speed internet access on Metro-North, and the Department of Transportation would fill that pothole.

I started to feel the tide turn and realized that knocking on doors was actually working. Voters who weren't in the mood to talk would sometimes follow up later and thank me for dropping by. "I'm the sweaty lady you met in Wilton the other day. I just want you to know that I'm rooting for you," one emailed.

As campaigns become increasingly consumed by digital advertising, some politicos have claimed that knocking on doors is antiquated and unnecessary. Maybe they're right, as President Biden's campaign won the largest number of votes in American history even after suspending their door-knocking operations for the majority of the campaign. But political intelligentsia may forget that the front doorstep is one of the last frontiers for candidates to learn about the electorate. Digital ads are great, but they don't tell you anything about the families who live in your district and what keeps them up at night. Candidates who forgo door knocking miss out on meeting voters who may not be very interested in politics but nonetheless have suggestions about how to make the community better.

Thankfully, I had plenty of company. What started with three seniors from Staples High School eventually grew into an internship program with dozens of high school and college students. Students across the state of Connecticut reached out to lend a hand, and we treated them as professionals. When I went door knocking with them, I learned what inspired them to get involved in politics, and I listened to their ideas about how to channel the National School Walkout movement into legislative action. Our campaign got a big break when the *New York Times* wrote about the race, and I was knocking on doors with Ava, an intern from Wilton, when the article came online. We blasted Ariana Grande and read the article out loud. Another afternoon, our intern Sam stopped me halfway down a driveway to tell me that Justice Kennedy was retiring. We commiserated together about what that would mean for the future of the U.S. Supreme Court.

While our opponent may have had decades of experience, our not-so-secret weapon was this army of teenagers who made sealing envelopes an extracurricular activity, and spent their summer calling the voters whose doors we didn't reach. These young people were involved in every aspect of our unorthodox campaign. For months, we ordered lunch and dinner from the pizzeria next door and worked together on the website, the policy platform, the press releases, and the tweets. When my car broke down in Ridgefield, Josh ran home to get some oil from his garage. Max from New Canaan didn't have his driver's license yet, and one day Jack spotted him walking almost a mile from the train station to our Westport office. Outside of the office, they were effective surrogates in school hallways and on social media. College students texted their friends to make sure they had requested, and then submitted, an absentee ballot. High school students hosted voter registration drives during their lunch hour and helped me send a personal letter to every single newly registered voter. One high school student who wasn't involved in our campaign messaged me on Twitter to let me know that he would try and get his parents to support me. Our campaign was powered by their energy and optimism, and it inspired volunteers of all ages. Students who weren't old enough to vote bonded with volunteers who had once voted for President Franklin Delano Roosevelt.

Some days, I'd pound the pavement with other Democrats who were on the ballot. Overlapping with the Twenty-Sixth Senate District was a handful of state representative districts, and they were almost all represented by Republicans. This year, those incumbents were being challenged by Democrats who underwent a similar political awakening after Trump's election. I was amazed that I'd made it onto the ballot alongside these qualified and passionate people. Anne Hughes, a social worker, was the gutsiest person I'd ever met. She would open up a front door if she heard someone inside who didn't answer the doorbell and introduced herself as their "future state representative." Anne was unapologetically progressive as she campaigned through a deeply Republican district. Stephanie Thomas was determined to knock on every single door in her district, even those that had her opponent's sign displayed in the front yard. Ross Tartell was often delayed on the trail by his knack for making friends with everybody we came across. He even managed to become friends with his opponent. Lucy Dathan put us all to shame with her door-knocking totals, carrying a set of prewritten "Sorry I missed you" notes so that no time was wasted if no one was home. Aimee Berger-Girvalo's top campaign staffers were her two kids, and while we knocked on doors together her son would skateboard alongside us. Raghib Allie-Brennan displayed patience when every voter mispronounced his name, and grace when his opponent hurled homophobic attacks his way. Although it was doubtful that many of us would win, we were newcomers and teammates as we navigated the complicated currents of local politics.

To be honest, I had little in common with these adult candidates who had been married or divorced, raised kids, or paid a mortgage. But now we found ourselves on an unlikely journey together, scrounging for food at meet and greets and practically memorizing one another's stump speeches. We texted constantly, and when my car broke down once again, Aimee popped open the hood and fixed it. If one of us was hosting a living room conversation, the others tagged along. We learned from one another, encouraged one another when the odds seemed steep, and vented about the length of these damn driveways. Most of all, we hoped to be working together soon at the capitol.

13

Apartment-gate

The opposition might not have been taking our campaign seriously, but it was clear that people in the community were starting to talk. "You're that kid my kid told me about" became a common refrain among fathers I met at the train station as the sun rose. Intrigued that Gen Z had arrived on the ballot, a local news station visited our campaign office and filmed volunteers licking envelopes. Then Sophie from *Westport News* shadowed me for a day and interviewed our interns and volunteers. Her article used the headline "Candidate Haskell Chases State Senate, History," which Meem gleefully cut out of the paper and stuck to her refrigerator.

As the local, state, and even national press became interested in our unusual campaign, reporters started to join me for a few hours of door knocking. It was a high-stakes proposition, as you never know who you'll encounter on the trail. For example, Jack invited Sandy from the *Aspetuck News* to join me for an afternoon of knocking on doors in Redding. There was plenty of time to kill as we meandered through Redding's windy roads, and she told me about her path to journalism, her love of running, and her fear of dogs. Silently, I worried that the fear of dogs might pose a problem. An hour later, we walked for a few minutes down a long driveway that led to a small cabin. I tapped on the front door, prompting several enormous dogs to bound out from around the corner. Sandy, indeed a runner, took off down the driveway before I realized what was happening.

I made plenty of mistakes with the press. I had no experience talking to reporters, so I often rambled on for too long about the historical voting trends of the district, precinct by precinct. Major outlets only wanted to talk about my age, and local outlets seemed scandalized that I dared challenge Boucher. One interview with the *Westport News* spanned the topics of voting rights, paid family leave, and how I felt I could help build a state that was more appealing to young people. I even chatted with the reporter in French. The quote they used? "I think years of bad experience is worse than no experience." That one didn't make it onto Meem's fridge.

The press was the only way Jack and I could follow the progress of Boucher's eerily silent campaign. When the *Westport News* shadowed Boucher for a day, we learned that she defended her vote against civil unions by stating that her LGBTQ constituents had asked her to vote that way. In a clip obtained by the *New York Times*, Boucher told a Republican crowd that I'd been endorsed by Congressman Himes and Senator Murphy because my parents were "wealthy donors to their campaigns." Jack and I quickly provided the reporter with documentation that my parents had never donated to any candidate, except for $20 that my mom had given to my campaign.

Compared to our open-door policy, Boucher's media strategy was basically to avoid reporters whenever possible. Eventually they started to take note. Tyler Pager from the *New York Times* wrote, "Last week, when *The Times* approached Ms. Boucher after her first candidate forum with Mr. Haskell, she said she had no time to talk because of another event she had to attend that evening. Ms. Boucher then lingered at the forum for at least another 15 minutes, chatting amiably with constituents and the other Republican elected officials who appeared at the forum."

Our media strategies couldn't have been more different. In fact, our campaign accepted some invitations that we should have turned down. One day in August, Jack and I trekked up to Danbury to tape a show for public-access television. The show was called *Progressive Soup*, and we knew nothing about it except that the host claimed to have plenty of viewers in Bethel. Our campaign wasn't gaining much traction in Bethel, and we figured there'd be lots of friendly questions since the word "progressive" was in the name of the show.

The host, a towering man with unkempt locks of gray hair and a long beard, met us at the door with a smile that seemed to say, "I can't believe you actually came." We made our way over to the set, which consisted of a table, two empty bowls, and two spoons. While we talked about politics, he encouraged me to pretend the soup bowl was full and mime a spoonful or two. Jack started to rub his head in his hands.

A quick note about Jack's telltale sign of stress; he suffers from such intense secondhand embarrassment that he is physically incapable of listening to bad speeches or fumbled toasts. This is a guy who can't watch *The Office* or any show that involves cringeworthy moments. His secondhand embarrassment peaked when a surrogate for the Lamont campaign arrived at an event and delivered a nonsensical and quite possibly inebriated speech. Jack was in the corner, nearly curled up in a ball and hiding his face in his hands. The habit drives me crazy, but I've come to accept that it truly is involuntary. Much to my chagrin, it's sometimes even anticipatory. At fundraisers, for example, Jack is so nervous that I might get the names of the hosts wrong that he stays in the back of the room, hands hovering near his head, until I've gotten past the thank-yous.

Once the cameras started rolling for *Progressive Soup*, I don't think Jack looked up from his hands more than once. The questions got goofier and goofier, and I thought back to the "yes, and" rule of improv. According to my high school theater teacher, actors needed to accept every premise and add something to it. If someone asks why you're riding a purple unicorn, you better come up with a name for the unicorn rather than deny its existence.

"Do you like your [imaginary] soup?"

"Yes, and here's why I believe it's time to raise the minimum wage."

"Hold that thought, I'm getting a message from my cat, Basil."

"Yes, and . . ." Basil, I learned, had died years ago. Our host wanted to use his time on air to communicate with the cat's spirit. When the interview wrapped up, Jack and I decided to be slightly more discerning about media requests. No cat séances seemed like a good start.

But fool me twice, shame on me. A few weeks later, we trekked up to the public-access studio one more time. This time, we were filming the *Marty Heiser Show*. Marty was a local Republican, but he was cohosting with a local Democrat. Most importantly, Boucher was also slated to appear, and this would be our first opportunity to share a stage. Unfortunately, we were in for another surprise.

Instead of finding Boucher in the chair across from me, I found Joe Visconti. Joe was running for the U.S. Senate, and although his campaign didn't gain much traction, he made some headlines when he referred to Connecticut's Asian American attorney general William Tong as Kim Jong Tong. Joe and I couldn't be more diametrically opposed, which he made clear when he started the segment by claiming that "Donald Trump [was] paving the streets of America with gold." For almost an hour, he lectured me about how the Democrats had been ruining the country since "long before [I] was born," and he ended the interview by throwing a rubber chicken across the table.

Jack and I were silent on the way home. I was disappointed that Boucher hadn't shown up, and felt like an idiot for falling into a trap. Although that was our last visit to the public access studio, we continued to say yes to nearly every other media request. In fact, we granted more access than ever before when the Republican Party filed a complaint against me in the week leading up to Election Day. Their claim? I was using campaign dollars to pay rent—a violation of Connecticut's elections law. "Will Haskell is showing us that he is too immature to run for office, using a scheme to live in an apartment on state money while families are struggling to pay their own rent," the press release read. "Moreover, Will is using the CEP grant as his own personal slush fund and I think the State Elections Enforcement Committee should look into this matter so abuses like this stop," Connecticut GOP chair J. R. Romano added. Unable to settle on just one lie, the Republicans were also circulating a video saying the apartment was merely a fake address, and I actually lived in my mom's basement.

I was shaking hands outside of Stop & Shop in Wilton when the CT GOP tagged me in a tweet. Among the many things that pissed me off about this complaint was the fact that I had to find out about it on Twitter. The local press started sharing the press release, as did other Republicans in town. One elected official in New Canaan posted an article on his Facebook page, raising the alarm that "if this is true . . . very troubling."

Of course it wasn't true. I was paying Jack a little over $1,000 a month, in accordance with the contract we had signed in March. He and I split the rent on our apartment each month, paying through our personal accounts. The Republicans were just making stuff up.

I knew I had done nothing wrong. But I also knew that perception could become reality. My mind was racing through a few nightmare scenarios, so I abandoned shaking hands outside the grocery store and drove to our Wilton office. Jack, pacing frantically, was trying to get a lawyer on the phone through the Connecticut Democratic Party. My phone started ringing with supporters who wanted to know if the allegations were true and reporters who wanted a comment from our campaign. Marge wanted to know what documents were needed to comply with the investigation.

I walked to the second floor of our office, a former spa with dozens of tiny massage parlors. I had four missed calls from reporters, and I decided to call back Heather Borden Hervé first. Heather published a blog called *Good Morning Wilton*, providing thousands of readers with updates from around town. Wilton was Boucher's home turf, so I figured there were plenty of voters there who might be skeptical of my candidacy. Plus, I trusted her to write a fair story.

She asked if she could come over and see the apartment, and perhaps even have dinner. She argued that opening up our home would allow Jack and I to demonstrate that we really lived there, and no campaign dollars were at play in paying our rent.

I called my brother, David, to see if that was too risky. Our apartment looked like a hurricane of dirty laundry had swept through it, and for some reason everything in the kitchen was sticky. Bringing a reporter to Burtis Avenue seemed like a big risk. David works as the editor of a magazine, and I figured he'd know how to handle a bad news cycle. When I told him the story, he laughed.

"That's a great idea. Just show people that you guys did nothing wrong."

I called Heather back, and she offered to come over for dinner that night after campaign events had wrapped up. She'd be there at 9 p.m. sharp.

We had two meet and greets that evening, but Jack skipped the second one so he could clean up the apartment before our guest arrived. I pulled into the driveway at the exact same time as Heather's blue jeep, emblazoned with a *Good Morning Wilton* magnet on the driver's door. I took a deep breath and braced myself for what we would find when we went upstairs.

Jack had done his best to hide piles of clothes under the bed and behind the couch. All the towels were hung up, which would be considered a win on a normal day. He had even started cooking peppers and sausage on the stove. He'd actually managed to make our cramped living room seem nice.

Heather brought a liter of Coke, and I poured drinks as she took a look around the room and chuckled. Here's how she described the scene in her article:

Their apartment is on the second floor of an older wood-frame house in the center of downtown New Canaan. There's a spa business on the ground floor, and an apartment upstairs.

There's one small bedroom which doubles as Lynch and Haskell's living room. It's neat and tidy, albeit crowded with a couch, coffee table, bunk beds, small shelves and a dresser. Framed pictures on the walls show the two roommates with friends from their college days. There's also a large poster of a fundraising thermometer—filled in at the party they threw with friends last spring at Georgetown when Haskell declared he was running for office. It tops out at $300.

For a first apartment right out of college, it's unremarkable save for the fact that it's pretty well-kept and clean. There are even throw pillows on the couch. There's food in the fridge—some orange juice, a large container of chicken noodle soup that a supporter left on their porch when both Haskell and Lynch were sick last week, and other basics. There are only two chairs at the small kitchen table, but real dishes, utensils and sundry pantry items. It's clearly furnished and lived in.

She snapped a few photos, thankfully sparing us a picture of the bunk bed. Meem would have been horrified that I hadn't made my sheets. Once we sat down for dinner, I shared my frustration about apartment-gate.

"Really? This is what they want to talk about seven days away from the election?" I was growing tired of the disbelief from many voters that young people could actually find a place to live in Fairfield County. More importantly, I was disappointed that a campaign focused on big ideas had been sidetracked by something so small. "I don't think that we should choose elected officials based on how many square feet they're sleeping in every night. Instead, we should choose them on their values and on their beliefs and on their ability and willingness to listen to their community," I said.

This may have been a cramped apartment, but that's what moving back to Connecticut looks like when you're twenty-two years old. The goal of my campaign was to encourage more people to do just that, so why hide the size of my living room? For that matter, I wasn't going to apologize for the fact that I didn't own property. After all, 34 percent of Connecticut households are rented. "Those voices deserve a representative in the state Senate, too," I told Heather. "I don't think that we need to go back to the days of only property owners in the legislature."

The article obviously didn't satisfy everyone. The Wilton Republican Town Committee released a statement saying that even if I hadn't broken the law, my living situation "shows lack of experience and judgment." Some members of a Democratic Town Committee called to say that the article made it look as though Jack and I were a couple. But I found the whole ordeal cathartic. Owning the fact that I was twenty-two and trying my best to figure out how to live here was a useful lesson that sometimes absolute transparency is the only way to change the topic. Reporters stopped asking about where I lived, and in the final week of the election we got back to talking about the issues.

14

Laughing at Myself, Smiling at My Opponent

Those who are running for president don't miss the Iowa State Fair or Jim Clyburn's South Carolina Fish Fry. Famously, presidential candidates descend on these events to kiss the babies and proverbial rings of voters who just happen to participate in the presidential primary contest before the rest of us. In the eyes of the campaigns and the national reporters who follow them, these events become a testing ground for candidates to prove they can go the distance. The handful of voters in attendance become bellwethers for the millions of voters who don't get the chance to share a corn dog with Pete Buttigieg or a pork chop with Amy Klobuchar.

Those who are running to represent Connecticut's Twenty-Sixth Senate District better not miss the *New Canaan Advertiser* Coffee. The *New Canaan Advertiser* is the town's weekly paper, and its editor moderates an off-the-record conversation every Friday morning with anyone who bothers to show up. Usually, the first selectman, state legislators, Board of Education chair, and Board of Finance chair are all on hand, along with the president of the library, plenty of local realtors, and a delegation from the New Canaan Men's Club. Like the early primaries, it's a time-honored proving ground.

New Canaan is one of the wealthiest towns in America, so one might wonder what sorts of problems could make these meetings so contentious. For weeks, this group will debate which material should be used on a stone wall outside a condo complex, or whether or not the plaster in the town library is a faithful re-creation of the plaster that was used in 1913. No news on the national stage, no matter how groundbreaking, can distract the group from their heated discussions about dog poop in Irwin Park or the number of available parking spaces on Main Street.

Shiva Sarram, New Canaan's tireless Democratic organizer, corralled a group of friendly faces to have my back at the very first coffee. I didn't understand all the fuss, since I was anticipating another group of adults who were skeptical of a young person running for office. But New Canaan was tougher territory than I realized. When I arrived, I sat next to an older woman wearing a cheery yellow sweater. When I stuck out my hand to introduce myself, she rolled her eyes and turned her back toward me.

Week after week, I kept going to the *Advertiser* Coffee. I greeted their skepticism with a smile and asked about their kids. Peter Hanson, a Democrat who had been attending the coffee for decades, advised me to speak louder and not wait to be called on. I became familiar with the debate over a cell tower's placement in town, and developed an opinion about whether or not the annual sidewalk sale should be allowed to shut down traffic on Main Street. Maria, a local Republican, disliked me so much that she couldn't even manage to fake a smile when I greeted her every Friday morning. At one particularly contentious coffee, she pointed out that she had kids my age, and her kids didn't pay property taxes, car taxes, or income taxes. "What have you done? What is your relevant experience?"

The *Advertiser* Coffee was often exhausting and demoralizing, but I tried to never miss it during the first few months of the campaign. I wanted to show this group that I could take whatever they threw at me, and I wasn't going to shy away from the fight. Central to the

Republicans' case against me was that I was still a kid, and therefore lacked whatever it took to be a state senator. But every once in a while I felt as though I were the adult in the room.

In September, Boucher posted on Facebook that four of her lawn signs had gone missing in Weston. "Not only is this immature child-ish behavior, it is against the law and authorities can investigate," she wrote.

I probably would have ignored the accusation if she hadn't used the word "childish." But that got under my skin, so I called Boucher and left a voicemail explaining that our campaign didn't steal lawn signs. Then we shared her post with a note: "I called Senator Boucher as soon as I saw this post. While we disagree on many issues, we're on the same page here. There is no room in this race for fighting over lawn signs. The issues are too important and the stakes are too high. I also asked her to call me directly if there are any additional reports of missing lawn signs—I'll drive over and replace them myself." The response on Facebook was overwhelmingly in our favor. We'd managed to look like the more mature campaign.

I figured out that campaigning involved a lot of taking whatever was thrown at me with a smile. When Jack McFadden, an unfail-ingly kind Democrat, invited me to volunteer at the Wilton Kiwanis German Festival, I figured I'd run into some grumpy Republicans. With the exception of a few Democrats like McFadden, the Kiwanis Club was filled with gentlemen of a certain age who yearned for the good ole days when Connecticut didn't tax their income. I hoped this would be a chance to make inroads with some of those voters while passing out schnitzel, or whatever. But when I arrived at the Wilton YMCA, an older gentleman in lederhosen met me at the entrance and told me to "scram." Apparently, there would be no tolerance for my politicking at this event. Although I told him that I had signed up to volunteer, he shook his head and shooed me away. A tad disappointed but content to go knock on doors instead, I got back in my car and drove away.

A few minutes later, McFadden called and apologized for his friend. He said that he'd smoothed things over and wanted to know if I'd be willing to work the French fry station. I was careful to leave all campaign stickers and flyers in my car when I returned, as to avoid any appearance of politicking. For the next few hours, I made a few friends while doling out extra portions of fries. Just as I was getting the hang of the fryer, I noticed the man in lederhosen walking in my direction. As he got closer, I saw the two shots of Jäger in his hand. After a few drinks and a bit of Bavarian dancing, he welcomed me to the event and I assured him there were no hard feelings. But as we took our shots, I spotted Boucher moving from table to table, handing out her campaign flyers. The rules are different for beloved incumbents.

The 2018 campaign cycle was a tough time to be a Republican in Connecticut. President Trump's first two years had been a disaster, and even these fiscally conservative suburbs were outraged by his order to separate families at the border and his insistence that there were good people on both sides of a confrontation with neo-Nazis in Charlottesville, Virginia. Republican elected officials were asked whether or not they supported the president, and their failure to answer spoke volumes louder than their uninspired pledge to lower taxes.

Perhaps recognizing the peril of an unpopular party leader, Republican campaigns became fixated on Connecticut's departing governor, Dan Malloy. Governor Malloy was leaving office that year with astonishingly low favorability ratings. He'd made difficult decisions during his eight years in office, including increasing the income tax rate and negotiating a deal with state employees to help pay down outstanding pension liabilities. Hoping to tie every Democrat on the ballot to the legacy of Malloy, Republicans started to send out mailers with photos of Democratic legislators standing next to the departing governor. Severely misreading the room, they thought people would be walking into the voting booth with the governor of Connecticut, not Donald Trump, on their mind. But when it came to our race, they faced a big problem: I hadn't met the governor. One benefit of running for office at a young age is that it was pretty hard to find skeletons in my closet. I didn't even have a closet to put them in.

Undeterred, they downloaded a stock photo titled "Cheerful Father and Son," and sloppily pasted Malloy's face on the father and mine on the son. I was out door knocking when a supporter called to say she had received the mailer. Although the text of the mailer seemed negative, she wanted me to know that I was looking stronger and taller since she'd last seen me. I knew that couldn't be true, so I asked her to text me a photo of what she had received.

To my amazement, I was depicted as taller than the over-six-foot-tall governor. Almost flatteringly, my face was pasted onto the tan and muscular "son." One of our interns found the original stock photo, and we decided to post it on Facebook to poke fun at the attempted smear. "There's a lot of craziness in the final stretch of this campaign, but the new mailing from my opponent is an all-time favorite," we wrote. It was an opportunity to make fun of myself, but also to remind people that our campaign was focused on the issues.

Running for office means making yourself vulnerable, and I often dealt with that by laughing at myself in the face of criticism. I'd be lying if I said I didn't spend hours stewing over the harsh comments that I saw on social media. Katie wondered why I wasted so much time reading through local Facebook groups, and I didn't have a good answer. It certainly wasn't a productive use of my time, and nasty nicknames from Facebook users I'd never even met hurt me. Publicly, I tried to look self-effacing and unscathed. I was new to politics, didn't have a mortgage, and owned only two suits. For all the hours that I dedicated to this campaign, I'd never be able to hide my inexperience. But if I could demonstrate maturity along the way, maybe I had an opportunity to swing a few voters my way. When the *Advertiser* Coffee crowd was particularly feisty, or the Republicans were particularly cruel on Facebook, I'd step back and think about the absurdity of the situation in which I found myself. I was running to represent a small corner of a small state. Most people didn't know who their state senator was, anyway. About two years ago, I was one of them. Soon, I'd likely be sharing a beer with friends, looking back on my strange expedition into suburban minefields. In the meantime, my campaign was focused on solving some real problems. I'd stay above the fray when I could, and greet punches with a smile when I couldn't.

15

Floppy Ears from the Land of Misfit Toys

At community events and on their front doorsteps, I noticed that many men of a certain age viscerally rejected my candidacy. To be sure, I connected with countless young people over social media who displayed the same enthusiasm I had seen at our dorm-room fundraiser; they wanted our generation to have a seat at the table. And at front doors, older voters often shook my hand and nodded in approval about passing the reins of leadership to the next generation. But middle-aged men weren't quite ready to let go of those reins. Maybe they didn't take me seriously because I was younger than their children, or maybe I didn't know how to act around conventional dad types. One thing was clear: the issues I talked most about—gun violence prevention and paid family leave—didn't resonate with them.

I knew I couldn't win this election without at least some of these suburban dads supporting my campaign, so we found some money to conduct a focus group. The session would focus on moderate male voters of the Twenty-Sixth District. Debra Stern and Nancy Carberry, local Democrats who were overqualified for the job, threw themselves into every detail of the process. They'd recently founded Carberry Stern Advisors, a consulting company to advise candidates, and they hoped to recruit ten men over the age of fifty who planned to vote, made more than $150,000 per year, and identified as politically independent or unaffiliated. They didn't want anyone who had strong feelings about Boucher, nor anyone who had heard of me before.

As it turns out, it isn't easy (or cheap) to lure a group of upper-middle-class men into a dreary market research center on the weekend. After a few weeks of calling strangers and offering them Amazon gift cards, Debra and Nancy finally had a group of nine guys ready to participate. These local dads were all over the map when it came to politics. When asked to name their most-admired politicians, they shouted out Donald Trump, Barack Obama, Ronald Reagan, Chris Murphy, and John McCain. The issues that mattered most to them were all fiscal, most notably pension funding, tax rates, and Connecticut's ability to attract businesses.

Jack had scheduled a meet and greet at the same time as the focus group, which meant I couldn't watch the conversation with the rest of our team from behind a one-way mirror. I was pissed, but in retrospect it was for the best. When I watched the tape the next morning, I felt like a new candy bar being picked apart by nine strangers. Debra's production of *Nine Angry Men* lasted roughly two hours, and she started the conversation by passing out a brief summary of my platform. The group generally supported my proposals to improve infrastructure, and they were eager to oust ineffective incumbents. They confessed that their wives usually told them who to vote for in state and local races, but they were certainly frustrated about the direction our state was headed. Before they had seen me, most of them could imagine voting for me.

But when Debra played my announcement video, they either laughed or quietly shook their heads. They felt they'd been duped. One participant said I looked like I was "from the land of misfit toys, with floppy ears." Katie liked that one.

They said I probably didn't have calluses. I hadn't started businesses.

I'd never had a real job. I lacked gravitas and probably didn't own an old T-shirt. My brain wasn't fully developed yet.

"That's a fact," one participant chimed in.

"But twenty-two-year-olds won World War II," another replied.

"When I was twenty-two years old, I couldn't tie my shoes," he responded.

"So you're comparing Will to yourself at twenty-two?" Debra probed.

"I'm just saying, we've got problems if we let millennials into politics," he replied.

"But look at what the baby boomers did," another shot back. I wasn't sure if he was praising all that the baby boomers had accomplished, or acknowledging everything that they had screwed up.

"Let's remember that the president needs to be thirty-five years old. The founders put some value in life experience."

Of course, our founding fathers were more like founding twenty-somethings at the time of the American Revolution. Nathan Hale, Connecticut's state hero, was twenty-two years old on July 4, 1776. More than a dozen signers of the Declaration of Independence were younger than thirty-five.

Interestingly, the men all perked up when Debra played a clip from a panel I'd appeared on alongside Boucher. They liked that I wasn't afraid to criticize her record and wanted me to do so in explicit terms.

"He should spend more time asking her why she hasn't gotten anything done. She's been in Hartford for more than a decade?" one participant asked. Grunts echoed around the table.

"That's a turnoff for me," another agreed.

With momentum seeming to build in our favor, Debra asked them to complete a few sentences.

"The most important trait of a first-time candidate is _____."

"Experience."

"The future of this country is in _____."

"Big trouble."

"The next generation of leaders need to _____."

"Grow some."

"It's on people our age to _____."

"Educate."

"Will's advantage is _____."

"His idealism."

"But life will take his idealism and turn it into realism," another countered.

None of this fared well for our campaign. Asked if they would consider voting for me, they mumbled "Probably not," before conceding that their daughters might. My jaw clenched when a few of them said they would consider supporting me if I had a chance of winning. I can't understand why so many voters want to pick a winner, as if there's some reward associated with voting "correctly." That sort of thinking creates a vicious cycle in which underdog candidates are summarily rejected under the guise of "electability."

Thankfully, there was some good news. "When I vote, I'm thinking about myself, but more than that, I'm thinking about my kids," one participant said. "Will needs to appeal to older folks by promising to represent the interest of their kids."

"Appeal to their maternal or paternal instinct," another agreed.

"This country is going to be his in twenty years. On that level, he kind of deserves some consideration," another added.

The camera kept rolling as the nine men got up to leave, and I heard them grouse about Debra serving soda rather than beer. They joked about "some young girl" who had just won a congressional seat in the Bronx. Watching the tape, I thought these must be the only voters in the country who didn't know Alexandria Ocasio-Cortez's name yet. When the clip ended, I started it again from the top. Watching myself be picked apart was really hard, and their comments demonstrated just how many challenges lay ahead. These grumpy, middle-aged men were omnipresent in the Twenty-Sixth District, and the very idea of my candidacy offended them.

But I wanted to learn from their criticism. If I could convince these voters that I was ready to learn, wouldn't back down from a fight, and would build a better future for their kids, maybe I could win over just a few. If we convinced them that this district was ready for a change, maybe they'd vouch for me on the golf course or at the water cooler.

How could we reach these guys in the coming months? Questionnaires they completed at the start of the session indicated that they spent their weekends on the sidelines of Little League games or at car shows. So I attended Caffeine and Carburetors in New Canaan, even if I didn't know how to drive a stick shift, and shook hands on the sidelines at local sports tournaments. One time, weeks after the focus group, I actually spotted one of the participants in Wilton. I wanted to introduce myself and ask him whether my ears looked as floppy in person, but Jack insisted I steer clear.

16

The Debates

Every weekday afternoon, our campaign headquarters transformed from a quiet office to a teeming hub of teenage energy. High school volunteers piled onto bean-bag chairs and competed over who could make the most phone calls. The headquarters, formerly a Chinese restaurant, consisted of one giant room. Even when we tried to build a makeshift office using cardboard boxes, there was never any privacy. Without any functioning walls, anyone who happened to be in the office could sit in on every meeting. If an intern showed up to pick up a new batch of lawn signs, they often stayed a while to participate in the budget debrief. If a new voter dropped in to learn more about my campaign, they might stumble upon a heated debate over what to include on our next mailer.

I walked into the office for our first day of debate prep with a yellow legal pad filled with chicken-scratch handwriting and zingy one-liners. The night before, I'd stayed up late writing responses to every possible question I might get from the moderator and rebuttals to every imaginable attack from Boucher. I hadn't been in my high school debate club, so I figured I better overprepare.

Maryli joined debate prep, and she brought in her deputy, Kevin Alvarez. Behind a thick beard, professorial glasses, and a wide smile,

Kevin hides an encyclopedic knowledge of Connecticut politics. At the University of Connecticut, he had risen through the ranks of both the College Democrats *and* the College Republicans, undoubtedly progressive but determined to foster dialogue between the two camps. He had approached his job in UConn's student senate with more seriousness than some politicians can muster for the U.S. Senate, and he knew the ins and outs of Connecticut's tax structure, transportation system, and higher education funding. Most important for today, he had developed a chameleonlike ability to channel Toni Boucher. Kevin had pored over every one of her previous debates and had watched her speeches in the Senate. He had memorized not only her political positions but also the position of her hands as she retold favorite stories. It was scary.

Debate prep mainly consisted of Maryli and Jack trying to surprise us with questions, and Kevin tearing me apart. In the actual debate, I'd be allowed to use two rebuttals. But during these rehearsals, I tried rebutting everything Kevin put out there. I wanted to figure out which rebuttals were the most effective and which responses I'd do better to ignore. And when it came to attacks, Kevin didn't go easy on me. I practiced smiling politely as he ripped into me for my lack of experience and asked me to define obscure state government terminology. He asked if I knew how to file taxes or which highway would bring me to Hartford. We knew Boucher was unlikely to be so confrontational, but it couldn't hurt to be ready.

Halfway through our first rehearsal, I got a call from Vin Mauro, the chief of staff for the Connecticut Senate Democratic Caucus. Maryli rolled her eyes at the interruption, but Vin is one of those people who you don't send to voicemail. Driving around in his pickup truck and yelling into a crackly Bluetooth connection, Vin told me that President Obama was going to endorse my campaign.

"I'm sorry, can you say that again?" I asked. He confirmed that I'd heard him correctly. I flipped to a new sheet on my legal pad and scratched out a note to the group: "OBAMA." God knows what else Vin said during the call—I couldn't hear much over Jack, Kevin, and the interns standing on their chairs and shouting at the top of their lungs.

President Trump may have angered me into running for office, but President Obama was the reason I had been drawn to politics in the first place. In 2007, his speech inside a high school gymnasium made me feel optimistic about the future of the country and intrigued about the promise of representational government. For eight years, I'd watched from my mom's living room as he fought for affordable health care, spearheaded a global commitment to reverse climate change, and brought our economy back from the brink of collapse. Now he was endorsing me? It didn't add up. My parents burst into tears when I called them.

Political consultants have a lot of bad days and a few good days, so I think they develop a survival instinct that prevents them from becoming too invested in any particular moment or campaign. Maryli certainly wasn't one to get swept up in emotion, and even the former leader of the free world couldn't distract her from the task at hand. She noted quietly that Obama would give our campaign some credibility—the understatement of the millennium—and signaled for us to all sit down and get back to work.

Happy to bring me down a peg, she told me I had to memorize everything on the legal pad. Reading from notes was a bad look for any politician, and it was especially perilous for a young candidate. Voters would think I was a puppet of the Democratic Party, reading prepared talking points from the likes of Nancy Pelosi. I needed to speak with a conviction and command of the facts that appeared spontaneous.

We learned pretty quickly that I wasn't great at providing succinct answers to complicated questions. When Jack lobbed a question about Metro-North, I used most of my time to talk about Wi-Fi rather than train speed. When Maryli asked about paid family and medical leave, I blabbered on about how America was an outlier among OECD countries, then paused to explain that OECD stood for Organisation for Economic Co-operation and Development. I ran out of time before explaining what paid family and medical leave actually was, let alone how it would make a difference in people's lives. Charlotte and Grace, two all-star interns who came into the office every day after school, grimaced at many of my ineffective responses.

So we practiced, and practiced, and practiced some more. Eventually, we had a new problem on our hands. After all this practice, my answers were starting to sound canned and inauthentic. One trick to sound more real, Kevin recommended, was to seem slightly annoyed. Hungry, tired, and eager to call my grandparents and let them know that President Obama would be endorsing me, I had no trouble sounding annoyed.

The next day was debate day, and I spent most of the afternoon knocking on doors by myself. Eager to think about anything other than thirty-second answers, I huffed and puffed through a hilly neighborhood in Ridgefield and reflected on how I had landed on this unusual path to politics. I remembered the sadness and anger I felt the morning after Trump's victory. I thought back to President Obama's farewell address—specifically his call for young people to roll up their sleeves and change a government that disappointed them. I'd taken him up on it, and unexpectedly, he'd had my back.

I was just starting off down another long driveway when my phone began to buzz about a tornado warning. Hoping to at least make it to the first debate in one piece, I went back to my car and drove over to the Ridgefield Public Library.

Since the debate wasn't starting for another half hour, I sat in my car for a while and watched a massive rain shower fall onto the parking lot. Nervous that I was about to make a fool out of myself, I tried to remember that I hadn't run for office because I believed I was the only or the best person to do this job. Nor was I motivated by a single issue like climate change or gun violence prevention. I'd run because I felt we were heading in the wrong direction on a host of issues, and I wanted to help correct the course. Our country had made a mistake in 2016, and the upcoming midterm was our first opportunity to fix it. As I had dug into the details of democracy, narrowed in on a race, and set my sights on breaking a tie, I'd successfully convinced my supporters that seats in the Senate don't belong to the people who happen to sit in them—they belong to the voters. Those voters have an opportunity to reevaluate their representation every two years and elect someone more closely aligned with their hopes for the future. Tonight I had to prove I was that person.

I looked up and saw Boucher, wearing her classic red pantsuit, walking into the library. When I made my way downstairs, I was shocked to find a packed house. My mom, Marge, a handful of friends, and about 200 strangers had braved the tornado and made it to the debate. Debra was sitting in the front row, reminding me with a not-so-subtle shake of her fist what she had learned from the focus group: be assertive. Behind her were voters of all ages who looked strangely excited for this rather esoteric debate.

The debate also included four state representative candidates, and we were all ushered to a back room to draw names out of a hat. Boucher drew number one and I drew number six, meaning we would be as far apart on the panel as possible. It felt like we both breathed a sigh of relief, as it might have been awkward to criticize the person sitting right beside you.

Kevin may as well have written Boucher's opening statement. He smiled from ear to ear in the audience as she borrowed his talking points about eliminating the income tax and reducing the size of government. She didn't look up from her notes as she criticized "some people" who support tolls. That would be me.

While the four candidates for state representative gave their opening statements, I thought back on all the hours of debate prep, plus my meandering thoughts from the parking lot. When it was my turn, I started speaking slowly and softly. One man in the back yelled out, "Louder!"

"I think not only our nation but also our state is at a crossroads," I said, moving my mouth closer to the microphone. "We're experiencing a moment of moral clarity. Our reaction can't be to reelect the same person who has been in Hartford year after year. Instead, I think it's time to try something new. It's time to send new voices into government and decide that Connecticut can do better."

Debates hosted by the League of Women Voters are sterile as a matter of policy. No claps or boos are permitted. As questions about pensions, transportation, taxes, and gun violence prevention were thrown at the panel, we each delivered succinct answers and dutifully passed the microphone to our right. Debra looked a bit disappointed that the format didn't allow for much direct confrontation with Boucher.

Our debate prep had been exhaustive and exhausting, so Jack, with his head in his hands at the back of the auditorium, knew just about everything I was going to say. But when we got a question about LGBTQ equality, I decided to veer from the script. I wanted to talk about my older brothers, and how I'd grown up without ever learning that there was something different about two boys holding hands or kissing. Beyond the quirky nature of my family, this sort of early-childhood exposure to and acceptance of the love of same-sex couples was uniquely possible for Gen Z. We had grown up in a more understanding world, even if only slightly so.

"I grew up in a family where gay just happens to be the norm," I said, prompting some puzzled looks from the audience. I explained how I revered my older brothers, and as I saw each of them marry their respective boyfriends, I learned at a young age "that family values apply to all families."

The audience actually applauded, giving me new confidence to speak on the fly. When it was my turn to deliver a closing statement, I ditched my talking points and looked at my mom in the audience. She was clearly nervous for me, avoiding eye contact at all costs.

"I began this campaign with just a few friends and neighbors, nervous that I was too young to make a difference. Having knocked on almost four thousand doors, having hosted one hundred fourteen meet and greets, and having earned the endorsement of President Barack Obama yesterday, I know that this campaign isn't about me. It's about all of our hopes for a better tomorrow than yesterday. And one voter at a time, we're going to show up this November, break the tie in the Senate, and move this state forward."

For the first time in over an hour, I unclenched my toes and felt my jaw relax. I'd made it through the first debate without saying billion instead of million, or tripping over the word "amortization." Thrilled to find a bar that was still open, Jack, Kevin, and I went out for a beer to laugh at my mistakes and think through the next debate. I felt like a cloud had lifted now that the first one was behind us. But Jack reminded me: four more to go.

In Wilton, Representative Tom O'Dea rose to Boucher's defense when I quoted her remarks concerning gun control. "I'm sorry, Will, if you keep attacking her like that, I'm going to call you out. Because you're wrong," he said. I could see his face turning red, like a football coach who didn't like the ref's call. "You graduated from college last May," he added.

Shockingly, the audience started to boo. In Boucher's hometown, they were actually sticking up for me. Faithful to the rules of decorum, the moderator snapped, "Cool it, audience," but the boos kept growing. Tom didn't make eye contact with me for the remainder of the debate.

Debra, always in the front row and not getting any better at the art of subtlety, shook her fist wildly when I sidestepped a fight about fiscal irresponsibility in Hartford. She'd looked similarly disappointed when I thanked Boucher for engaging in a civil exchange of ideas. So, bolstered by the boos, I turned to Representative O'Dea and spoke off the cuff.

"Tom, with all due respect, you don't need twenty-two years of legislative experience to know that students should feel safe in the classroom. You don't need twenty-two years of legislative experience to know that we can't continue kicking the can down the road instead of addressing our pension liabilities head on. . . . It's time for all of us to take part in a government that belongs just as much to you and me as it does anyone else sitting on this stage tonight."

In my experience so far, politics hadn't entailed much ad-libbing. But in this moment, I felt like I had finally gotten to say exactly how I felt. It drove me crazy that Republicans were trying to blame me for decades of poor decisions in Hartford, then arguing in the very same breath that I wasn't ready for the job. Which was it—had I just graduated from college, or was I responsible for this legacy of financial mismanagement? They talked endlessly about the past, but I wanted to talk about the future. I didn't think we could build the next twenty years of prosperity by relitigating the last twenty.

With that off my chest, I started to actually enjoy the debates. I even crashed a debate that I hadn't been invited to. The Connecticut Realtors had formed a political action committee that was spending tens of thousands of dollars to defeat Democratic candidates, so claiming that my invitation had been lost in the mail was a comparatively minor insult. Funnily enough, the USPS had also dropped the ball for Julie Kushner, another Democrat running for a neighboring state Senate seat. We both arrived anyway, and she had the guts to stand up to the organizers and demand equal time as her opponent. The crowd was unfriendly, but at least Julie and I had an opportunity to speak for ourselves. One voter asked why I was challenging Boucher, and I launched into a list of policy disagreements. She looked confused. "But we love Toni," she replied.

At the debate in Redding, my opponent didn't show up. Incumbents are famous for trying to limit debates—some long-serving state senators don't debate with their opponent at all. I appreciated that Boucher had been willing to engage in so many debates, but it seemed like a miscalculation to skip the Redding League of Women Voters forum. Without an opponent on stage, I spoke freely about my platform without the jittery nerves I felt whenever she was nearby.

Even when we did share the microphone, I was learning to loosen up a little. At Westport's environmental forum, I was the only candidate to fess up that I hadn't completed a home energy efficiency inspection. "I share a small apartment where we can't actually control the thermostat," I explained, which got a few laughs. Kevin had spent all day drilling me with arcane environmental questions, so I was well prepared to talk about renewable energy sources and the state's water plan. But when another candidate was asked how young people could protect the environment, he recommended we all kayak more often. I almost spit out my water. Maybe I could do this job after all.

The final debate took place in Westport's town hall, inside the same auditorium where I had been nominated just a few months earlier. When I walked in, I saw my family sitting in the back row. Next to them sat Katie's family, including her grandmother, who had driven all the way down from Hartford. When I reached the stage, I realized I was as jittery as I'd been at the first debate. Seeing so many familiar faces in the audience brought on new anxieties.

Jack was also panicking, not because of the crowd but because the League of Women Voters had invited each candidate to submit a question for their opponent. We had prepared for Boucher's worst:

"Have you ever paid income taxes?"

"What's the average price of a home in Fairfield County?"

"Define fringe benefit and debt service ratio."

"What does SEBAC stand for, and what is the size of Connecticut's current budget deficit?"

We'd also spent a week bouncing around potential questions to ask Boucher. I wanted to know whether or not she had voted for Trump, but Kevin had spent so much time impersonating her that he was certain she would obfuscate, pointing out the sacred secrecy of the ballot. Our campaign had publicly criticized her votes to weaken vaccine requirements, eliminate publicly financed campaigns, and repeal the earned income tax credit. Surely she'd walk into the debate with ready answers to all of those critiques, so we needed to branch out and try something different.

It had been only a few weeks since the U.S. Senate had voted to confirm Brett Kavanaugh to the U.S. Supreme Court, willfully ignoring a history of sexual assault brought to light by Dr. Christine Blasey Ford. The compelling hearing had prompted many of us to have overdue conversations about consent, but it hadn't persuaded the U.S. Senate. Our Westport office proudly displayed a "Kava-nope" sign in the front window, and I joined Westporters on the Ruth Steinkraus Cohen Bridge to support Dr. Ford and other survivors who have been dismissed and maligned rather than believed and supported.

Of course, I was running for a seat in the state Senate, not the U.S. Senate. But state law governs sexual conduct and misconduct, and I wanted to continue the conversation about consent even if Justice Kavanaugh had his lifetime appointment on the bench. Late one night, I leaned over the railing of the top bunk and woke Jack up.

"I found it," I said. He looked confused and annoyed that I'd interrupted his sleep. In 2016, Connecticut had passed a law requiring colleges in Connecticut to enforce an "affirmative consent" standard on college campuses. Boucher had voted nay. Voters already knew that Republicans in Washington were not standing with survivors, and now we could effectively make the case that Republicans in Hartford were not standing with them either. I'd just stepped off a college campus where students fumbled with the nuances of sex and consent every Friday night. None of these issues were easily solved, but I believed in setting a baseline of respect and agency to give the next generation of eighteen-year-olds someplace to start.

In order for the question to land, we had to succinctly remind the audience what affirmative consent actually meant. So we defined it in the question. Our submission read: "You were one of twelve senators who voted against affirmative consent, which requires consent be given in an active, clear, and voluntary manner. Which one of these adjectives did you find objectionable?" Jack was in the fetal position by the time the moderator reached the end of the question.

It was clear we had caught Boucher off guard. She pivoted to LGBTQ rights, then talked about her work to bolster school security after the Sandy Hook tragedy. She said we didn't give her enough credit for working across the aisle.

Of course, Boucher was right. She wasn't the most conservative member of the state Senate, and she had worked with Democrats on some important initiatives. And it was true that our campaign didn't give her credit for that work. Winning this election required drawing contrasts and focusing on the dozens of objectionable votes that otherwise might have flown under the radar. I dug into her committee work, bringing to light her vote against penalties for distracted driving and her party's proposal to cut funding for the University of Connecticut. Our campaign had characterized Boucher as irredeemable, when obviously she was more complicated than that. I wanted to win, and I knew politics required confrontation. That said, I felt a twinge of regret when Boucher stumbled through an answer to our question.

After the debate, Boucher's supporters would claim that I had used my question to attack her character. My question had everything to do with policy and nothing to do with personal attacks, but I understood that it just felt too mean. A few days away from the election, I'd learned the limits of confrontational politics.

Sadly, I couldn't stick around to hear what my family thought, as I was scheduled to speak with a group of businessmen in Ridgefield that evening. As Jack reminded me, I needed to hit the road right away to make it in time for the end of their racquetball game. Sometimes, Fairfield County really is a caricature of itself. As Jack and Kevin walked me to my car, I mentioned how relieved I was to have these debates behind us. But as I got in the driver's seat, it occurred to me that my dad was still inside the auditorium. He was unpredictable in moments like this, so I asked Jack to keep an eye on him.

A few minutes later, my worst fears were confirmed. Along the rainy drive to Ridgefield, I got word from Jack, my mom, and my stepmom that my dad had cornered Boucher, and the two of them were deep in conversation. No one could seem to pull him away.

I was so furious that I almost ditched the racquet crew and turned my car around. Nothing in the campaign had made me feel so small and immature as having my father talk to my opponent. My dad had a habit of falling in love with whoever he happens to be talking to and, astonishingly, Boucher was no exception. She told him that the criticisms levied by my campaign were baseless, and powerful interests in Hartford were feeding me misinformation. She told him that after the campaign was over, she'd like to take me out to coffee and set the record straight.

When my dad called to tell me all of this, I felt crushed. Boucher thought so little of me that she was basically telling on me to a parent. And Dad's reaction, rather than sticking up for me, was to believe her and shuttle the message back. My team of interns had done the research on Boucher's voting history. I came prepared with bill numbers and roll-call votes, and I didn't know any powerful players in Hartford. I worked hard to appear independent from my parents, and I almost never allowed them to come to campaign events. Mom would occasionally bring a few of her friends to a phone bank, but I made sure that she didn't let anyone know we were related. But, like any twenty-two-year-old, I wanted my parents to be proud of me and to believe in what I was doing. Didn't my dad understand that when Boucher offered to take me out for coffee after the election, she was presuming that she would still be a state senator and I would be an apologetic former opponent?

The next day, I received a call out of the blue from a woman named Shirley. She was a Westport resident who wanted to know if I was related to Chev Haskell. Chev was my father's father, and he had died long before I was born. While I'm in near-constant contact with my three living grandparents, I know almost nothing about Chev.

When I confirmed to Shirley that I was Chev's grandson, she squealed with delight. Many decades ago, she and her husband had been close friends with Chev and my grandmother. She'd recently read about my campaign in the paper and offered to host a coffee for me. I was still mad at my dad, but I invited him to come along.

Dad arrived late and missed Shirley recounting stories about my grandfather. I learned that Chev had been a Republican chair on the Board of Education, and that he spoke precisely and listened intently. She showed me his favorite place to sit in her living room and told stories about their long dinner parties. Eventually, she led me to another room and invited me to give a short speech to a dozen friends who had gathered.

I delivered the same stump speech that I'd already given four times that day, but my mind was racing with questions about my grandfather. What would a Republican businessman have thought about his grandson running for office as a progressive? According to family lore, he was a moderate who felt abandoned by the Republican Party when they re-nominated Nixon. How might he have felt when they nominated Trump? He had died when he was fifty-five and my father had been a young man himself. His marriage had collapsed spectacularly, and toward the end of his life, my father was so angry at him that they barely spoke. Fathers are imperfect, but I had one who was only a few feet away, proudly listening to my stump speech. When I reached the end of my speech, I saw him smiling. With Shirley mingling through the crowd and sharing more stories about my grandfather, my dad and I hugged. Without missing a beat, he dove back into his usual list of suggestions about how my speech could have been better.

17

November 6, 2018

I jumped up at the clanging of my 4:30 a.m. alarm, forgot that I was on the top bunk, and slammed my head into the ceiling. It was Election Day, and I hoped the day would only get better from here. In the kitchen, I flipped on the lights to wake up Liam and Emily, the same friends who had helped us move into the apartment. They finally climbed off the air mattress by 5 a.m., by which time Jack was on the phone fielding requests from interns to deliver hundreds more lawn signs. The Republicans must not have slept at all, instead spending all night planting a sea of signs at every polling location. The sun hadn't yet risen, but already our team of high school and college students wanted reinforcements. I've never met anyone who decides which candidate they'll support by looking at how many lawn signs are stationed around the parking lot, but our team didn't want to come in second place in anything today. Jack sped off to grab more lawn signs, and I hopped in the back of Liam and Emily's car to visit our first voting location.

Despite the chaotic start to the morning, I felt calmer than I had in months. Finally, I stopped bracing myself for attacks. I could forget my stump speech and the arcane facts and figures I'd memorized. The fieldwork was done.

This district had 70,582 registered voters, and given the press surrounding the Trump administration, we projected about a 3 percent increase in turnout compared to the last midterm election in 2014. That amounted to 61.08 percent, or 43,114 voters. In order to win, we needed 21,558 people to circle the bubble next to my name.

Since May, we had been contacting a carefully selected group of voters who we believed could be persuaded to vote for me. The national Democratic Party compiles data on every voter in the country: that data is distilled into a handful of scores, including a support score that represents the voter's likelihood to vote for a Democratic state Senate candidate, and a turnout score that represents their likelihood to vote at all. We used this data to build a list of voters to target: women who had voted in all of the last three elections and had a support score that fell between 30 percent and 70 percent. Painfully aware after the focus group that men were harder to win over, our list criteria were more stringent about male voters and included only those who had voted in all of the last three elections and had a support score that fell between 40 percent and 70 percent. We added to the list all Democrats and unaffiliated voters under the age of twenty-four, all Democrats and unaffiliated women who had registered since President Trump took office, and a few other groups that we felt gave us a strategic advantage. That pool amounted to 25,751 people. After months of working through that list, we set it aside in the final days of the campaign and shifted to shoring up our base. That meant reaching out to voters with a support score higher than 90 but a turnout score lower than 60.

By Election Day, we had made over 30,000 phone calls and knocked on over 10,000 doors. Our team made contact at roughly 30 percent of those doors and on 12 percent of those calls, resulting in 8,081 actual conversations. As impressed as I was by our volunteers, the data they had collected wasn't exactly inspiring. Even among voters with a support score of over 90 percent and a turnout score of over 90 percent, only about 60 percent had pledged to vote for me.

I knew we didn't have to win in every town, but we had to keep our margins small in the towns that we'd lose. Figuring that we'd come up short in Boucher's hometown of Wilton and in the Republican stronghold of New Canaan, we had to pull off a major victory in my hometown of Westport. Things were looking good there—of the 8,081 voters we spoke to during the campaign, 2,019 lived in Westport. Redding and Weston were likely to go our way, but they were tiny towns compared to Ridgefield and Bethel. In order to win the race, we had to capture at least one of those big towns and keep the margin tight in the other. Jack and I had learned a great deal about data analytics and voter outreach over the last few months, but I still figured that I probably wouldn't win.

Some of that pessimism may have stemmed from sheer exhaustion. Regardless of the outcome, I was ready to resume sleeping late, spending time with Katie, and eating lunch again. I was tired of staying on script and worrying about whether I'd left a good impression on each and every person I met.

When Liam pulled into East Ridge Middle School in Ridgefield, the parking lot was already nearly full. Voters, presumably commuters at this hour, were waiting in their cars for the polls to open. This looked like more than a 3 percent turnout bump.

For the next fourteen hours, Liam and Emily kept me company as I thanked voters and silently wondered who they were there to support. Some wouldn't make eye contact with us, conveying the same sheepishness as a dog that had been caught chewing on the furniture. But other voters stopped to introduce me to their children or ask for a sticker, so there was some hope.

As we traveled between precincts throughout the day, Senator Chris Murphy, Congressman Jim Himes, my newborn niece Mimi, and a few other VIPs joined us for an hour here or there. I barely noticed when it started to rain, nor when it got dark out. With months of work behind us culminating on a single day, I didn't want a second to go to waste. When the polls finally closed at 8 p.m., I hugged Katie and my family in the parking lot of Saugatuck Elementary School. I thanked them for staying with me to the bitter end, and I felt two years of stress lifting off of my shoulders. My brother Stephen laughed about the Republicans who had scowled at him and shared predictions about the precincts he had worked that day, based only on the occasional thumbs-up or thumbs-down from a voter on the way out. My brother John took off my suit jacket and replaced it with the warmer jacket he had been wearing. Win or lose, it was time to celebrate a hard-fought campaign with the people I loved.

The Westport DTC had rented a local bar for the night, but I asked my closest friends to gather at my mom's house beforehand. I was nervous about getting the results in front of a big crowd, and Jack hoped we'd know the results in an hour, then head to the bar.

Boy, was he wrong. In the stress of the day, we had forgotten to position a volunteer at each precinct to collect results. That meant we were at the mercy of the glacial pace of the secretary of state's website. My brothers hovered around Jack's laptop in the kitchen, trying to extrapolate from one precinct or another. By 9 p.m., Jack pulled me aside and said we probably wouldn't know the results for many more hours. He suggested we head over to the party.

Packed with anxious Democrats and almost certainly in violation of fire codes, the bar was a frenzy of supporters and reporters asking for "comments on the results." There wasn't much to comment on, since I didn't know the results. So I made my way around the room, marveling at the mixing and matching of people in my life. Katie and Marge shared a tequila shot with septuagenarians from a DTC. Friends from college took over the dance floor while our interns paced nervously and looked for some food. My phone was unusable, with over 600 text messages asking the same unanswerable question—any numbers? I gained tidbits of information as I walked through the bar. Wilton was predictably going for Boucher, but we had pulled off a narrow win in Ridgefield (6,596 to 6,135). The *New York Times* had us behind, but *News 12* had us ahead. Westport came through in a big way, delivering a 28.42 percent lead over Boucher. But we got clobbered in New Canaan, coming in almost 16 points behind Boucher. My brother David filled me in on the national races: Democrats had won the House, but the Senate races were a wipeout. A live band was blaring music, making it hard to process any of this.

Mercifully, Kevin pushed his way through the room to pull me and Katie outside. When we reached the parking lot, Jack told us we'd narrowly lost Bethel and won Redding. We were looking at over 50,000 votes cast, meaning turnout had increased by double digits since the last midterm. Amazingly, it all came down to the tiny town of Weston. Blake, the data mastermind behind our campaign strategy, jumped in his car and raced to Weston's town hall. The crowd in the bar got the sense that something was happening, and a few of them came out to the parking lot to ask if there was any news. My brothers locked arms and formed a wall to give Jack, Kevin, Katie, and me some privacy. Maryli called to say that she thought we had won. She'd looked over the numbers, and Boucher would have to win an unreasonably high percent of the vote in Weston in order to squash our lead.

I saw tears building up in Katie's eyes and squeezed her hand. Believe it or not, we had never actually discussed what would happen if I won. Whenever she tried to bring it up, I changed the topic and said I didn't want to jinx anything. Now I realized that my habit of avoiding difficult conversations had been incredibly unfair to Katie.

I pulled her behind the bushes to get some distance from the others. She was in her first semester at Harvard Law School, so we hugged, cried, and promised each other that Hartford wasn't so far away from Cambridge. As I was stammering something about how we still didn't have the Weston totals back, I got a call from Toni Boucher.

"Will? I just wanted to congratulate you on your victory," said a now-familiar voice on the other end of the phone. "It's a big responsibility, and I hope you'll take it seriously." I thanked her for her many years of service. We each made empty promises about getting together for coffee sometime. I thought back to all of the hours I had spent watching her votes in college and preparing for debates once I'd come home. I couldn't quite believe she was conceding.

When we emerged from the bushes, Katie and I were swept up by the crowd. Someone put me on their shoulders and carried me into the bar. I gave a short speech, and the band agreed to play for another hour. Katie ordered more tequila shots. I hugged my family members who had come from far and wide to support me. At one point, I even saw my parents dancing together.

We stayed up so late that night that some of my friends went straight to work in Manhattan the next day. Our intern Josh Instagrammed a collection of photos he'd taken along the campaign trail. The caption read, "11/6/2018: A group of kids from across the 26th pulled off the impossible and became a family." We danced and I shrugged off questions about when I'd start this new job, where I would live, or how much I would make. I'd been so busy with the campaign that I hadn't bothered to think through any of those things. In the car on the way to the afterparty, I got a call from Senator Chris Murphy. I idolized Murphy, who was the youngest member of the U.S. Senate when he was elected at the age of thirty-nine. I'd knocked on doors for him before I was old enough to drive. Now, implausibly, he was calling me on my cell phone to say he was proud of me.

It was only after the party was over that I became paralyzed with fear. Lying in bed the next morning, I realized I had no idea what it meant to be a state senator. I'd spent so much time campaigning for this job, I hadn't stopped to consider whether I was actually up to it. Would my new colleagues take me seriously? I'd learned how to knock on doors and survive a debate, but I never learned how laws are written or passed. In just a few weeks, I would be responsible for representing about 100,000 people. Tens of thousands of them hadn't voted for me, and more than a few were expecting me to fail. What if they were right?

I rolled over and saw that Katie was crying. This relationship would be long-distance for a little longer.

"I don't know if I can do it," I said. "I haven't even started and I'm exhausted."

I'd spent half a year bouncing around these seven suburbs at a breakneck pace, a walking anachronism as I made small talk at cocktail parties with voters in my grandparents' generation. In addition to worrying about whether I could handle the substantive responsibilities of this job, I wondered if this was going to be a normal and healthy life.

Katie reminded me that this was an opportunity. I had just been given a front-row seat to the fight against climate change, the push for college affordability, and so much more. "There's a reason I voted for you," she mumbled.

The thought of changing out of pajamas and putting on a suit was nauseating. Still, Jack had committed me to a lunch in Bethel to thank some volunteers. He'd also set up two television interviews outside the event, and he promised that I'd be done after that. On the long drive to Bethel, I drilled down on what sort of state senator I would actually be.

I wanted to be accessible. I'd grown up not knowing that I even had a state senator. I wanted constituents to know that state government was there to help, and that I could be their advocate. During the campaign, I'd given out my cell phone number in our very first ad. I saw no reason to stop doing so now.

I wanted to take my constituents along with me on this unusual journey. I needed to learn the nitty-gritty details of passing laws in Hartford, and perhaps others would want to know what I discovered along the way. I hoped to use social media to provide a look behind the scenes, and I would work to make sure I spent just as much time communicating with younger constituents as I did older constituents. I wanted to prioritize visiting classrooms and talking with young people about their hopes for the future and how the government could help them along their journey.

I also wanted to be substantive. State politics is filled with people who only show up for a photo op, but I found those superficial events to be a waste of time. I wasn't old enough to seamlessly schmooze at PTA functions or wealthy enough to pay the entrance fee to fundraiser upon fundraiser. Instead, I wanted to host town hall meetings and discuss real policy issues. Perhaps most importantly, I knew I didn't want to be a state senator for the rest of my life. That decision was freeing. It meant I could make a politically unpopular decision when the moment required. Finally, I'd spend time with Katie, even if it meant driving all the way to Massachusetts just for dinner.

PART II

18

Freshman Orientation

Shortly after Election Day, I started to have a recurring nightmare.
I found myself in the cockpit of a commercial plane packed with
passengers, responsible for safely piloting their flight. I cranked the
engine, pushed some buttons, and actually managed to get the plane
off the ground. The passengers cheered, and we all celebrated while
cruising at around 30,000 feet. But as we approached our destina-
tion, I realized that I had no idea how to land the plane. How was I
expected to bring a heap of metal, racing through the sky, to a complete standstill on the ground? I'd begin to panic, struggling to figure
out the right speed with which to approach the runway. Invariably,
the plane exploded on impact and I woke up with a start.

In the weeks before I was sworn in, I set off driving all around
the state to meet my new colleagues and learn how they had landed
the plane. I wanted to know the minute details about life in the
legislature, like how to write a bill and how to access my new email.

In Danielson, I met Senator Mae Flexer, a natural ally. From the
booth of a diner in her district, Mae told me that she had been elected
to the House of Representatives in her twenties and understood how
overwhelming it was to be a young legislator. Now in her thirties,
she'd grown up in the capitol building and seemed genuinely thrilled

that I'd be joining her in the caucus room. For years, she had struggled to get other lawmakers to pay attention to the issues that impacted young people. Mae represented more students than any other senator, since her district included the University of Connecticut, Eastern Connecticut State University, and Quinebaug Valley Community College. We started strategizing about how to make college more affordable, and Mae shared tips about where to park and which colleagues could be trusted. She was also the only one frank enough to warn me: surviving on a senator's salary isn't easy. Senators made about $30,000 a year, plus some gas reimbursements. For roughly a decade, Mae had struggled to afford her mortgage. She knew the challenge would be even greater in my district, where median home values were more than 3.5 times higher than in her district.

In West Hartford, Senator Beth Bye seemed giddy about my age and greeted me with a big hug at her front door. Beth was immediately generous with information about which committees I should request and how Connecticut's budget is written. Unlike many of the politicians I had encountered, she seemed to have struck a reasonable balance between her personal and professional lives. She lived just a few minutes from the capital with her wife, Tracy, whom she had married on the first day that same-sex marriage became legal in Connecticut. Beth advised me not to take nasty emails from constituents to heart and reminded me that politics should never be considered a dirty word. As I stood up to say goodbye, she handed me a plaque that read, "You don't have to be crazy to work here. We'll train you."

That training started right away. Just a few days after the election, the Democratic state senators gathered in an otherwise-empty Italian restaurant in Hartford to mingle and elect the leaders of our caucus. Senator Marty Looney, the Senate president who was first elected to the General Assembly in 1981, proudly raised his glass to the twenty-three Democratic senators.

That is, until Jorge Cabrera was tapped on the shoulder by a bearded man with a grim look on this face. In a recount, Jorge had just lost his lead and fallen seventy-seven votes behind. Not quite as seasoned in the highs and lows of politics as my new colleagues, I was devastated that Jorge had literally lost his seat before our eyes. Nevertheless, we raised our glasses to the *twenty-two* Democratic senators. I made my way around the room and introduced myself to my new colleagues, and Mae was nice enough to vouch for me when one thought I was playing some sort of prank.

A few weeks later, freshman orientation started. It reminded me of the first few days of college. The new legislators and I made small talk as we got our IDs and furiously took notes about how a bill actually becomes a law. I documented the whole day on my Instagram story, excluding only the security briefing from the State Capitol Police. Many of the people who had knocked on doors for me or hosted a meet and greet at their house had no idea what it actually meant to be a state legislator. We'd learn together, I decided, and that started with providing a behind-the-scenes look at this unusual onboarding process.

It seemed at first like the freshman senators had nothing in common. Norm Needleman worked as the CEO of a major company that made fizzy pills like Alka-Seltzer tablets. Julie Kushner was a nationally known leader of the United Auto Workers, and she'd spent a career lobbying legislators to enact pro-worker reforms. Christine Cohen owned and operated a bagel shop with her husband. Mary Daugherty Abrams taught special education for twenty-five years before eventually retiring as a high school assistant principal. Saud Anwar, the first Muslim to serve in the state Senate, worked as a doctor specializing in lung diseases. I first witnessed his kindness and grace when he laughed off pepperoni pizza being served at his welcome party. Alex Kasser, whose district bordered mine, was a lawyer on the verge of wrapping up her PhD at Yale, and she walked into the building with a detailed plan to address nearly every one of Connecticut's problems. James Maroney and Matt Lesser had previously served in the state House of Representatives, so they were more like sophomores.

Although they skipped some orientation events, they made time to tell us which food to avoid in the cafeteria.

In ways both large and small, I felt a world apart from my new colleagues. During our meeting with human resources, one new senator asked which dental plan was advisable if their kids needed braces. I wanted to know which plan to choose if I hadn't been to a doctor since my pediatrician. When the conversation turned to salary, one colleague offered to forgo their salary. I asked for specifics about when it would arrive in my bank account. More substantively, they walked into the building with a bill drafted, or a lifetime of experience, or both. I arrived with a vision and some talking points from the campaign trail, and I found myself tongue-tied when one new colleague asked me a basic question: "What are you looking to get done here?"

Thankfully, we bonded during orientation. What brought the freshmen together wasn't a shared policy platform or similar personal lives, but instead the enormous stress we each felt as we tried to live up to the promises we had made on the campaign trail. Since Connecticut's General Assembly meets only from January to June, we needed to condense into six months what other legislators accomplish over the course of a year. We'd need to memorize the arbitrary, sacrosanct, and breakneck deadlines, the first of which was January 18th. That was our last day to file any bill, despite the fact we had only been sworn in nine days earlier. The first few weeks of session would be spent working in committees—we'd each serve on about five and chair one. As a committee chair, we would need to decide which of the hundreds of bills referred to the committee should be prioritized, then draft them in a way that would earn the approval by a majority of committee members. In a few months, we'd start meeting in the Senate chamber to amend and eventually pass those bills. But if a bill hadn't been approved in both the Senate and the House when the clock struck midnight on June 5th, it died unceremoniously. Legislating was a fast-paced and messy process, but we needed to master it quickly. Our freshman group text became a refuge for all sorts of questions: What's an A committee versus a B committee? Was anyone else having issues getting in touch with the Republicans on their committee? What did it mean to rise for a point of personal privilege? In what felt like a crossover between *The Breakfast Club* and *Veep*, we became an unlikely but close group of friends.

Before we were officially sworn in, we practiced using the lofty vernacular of the legislature. The procedural jargon, impossible to remember but critical to get right, was laid out in a little script that we tucked into our desks. That way, we'd remember to "move adoption of the amendment and ask to waive the reading." Then, "seek leave of the chamber to summarize." Whatever that meant. Ms. Ellaneous, who once toured my dad and me around the capitol building, gave the very same tour to our group of new senators. "Remember these details," she told us. "You'll need something to say when school groups come to visit you."

One night during orientation, I was invited out for a cigar by Vin, the chief of staff of our Senate Democratic Caucus. Always ready with an off-color joke and a solution to whatever problem you're facing, Vin is a fixer who relishes the process of cutting a deal. Politics ran in his family, too, and Vin's father had once led the Democratic Party in the city of New Haven. Now that job was Vin's, and he had served as Marty Looney's right-hand man for decades. Since Marty had risen in the ranks to the job of Senate president, Vin was the highest-paid state employee in the capitol. He had a higher salary than the governor, and he was much scarier. I choked a bit when he chided me for holding my cigar like it was a joint. But Vin is exactly who you want to have your back during a fight.

I tried to look natural with my cigar as Vin shared tips about how to get by in the legislature. "If you're in trouble, I'm the first person you call. Not your girlfriend, not your parents, not your lawyer," he told me. When a few beat cops stopped in to the bar, they rushed over to give Vin a pat on the back. Vin told me that my first reelection would be the toughest, and he promised to help me deliver some wins for my district in the coming months. He also advised that I avoid the capitol building unless I absolutely had to be there. "The fastest way to spot a legislator who is going to lose their next election is to see who is sitting in their office," he warned. Legislators should be seen around their district, attending Eagle Scout ceremonies, hosting roundtables, or cutting ribbons. In the months that followed, I'd hear Vin's voice in the back of my head as I hightailed it to my car after the last vote was cast.

Vin's list of dos and don'ts were mainly don'ts. Don't believe anyone, especially members of the House. Don't get married too early. Don't go to strip clubs. Don't go to any bars in Hartford. "The capitol types might seem like your friend, but they'll want something from you eventually. Don't trust them."

I took most of Vin's advice, but I soon met one capitol type I could trust without question: Alex Romanowicz. Every senator had their own legislative aide, and I had initially hoped to hire Jack. Many of my colleagues were hiring folks who had worked on their campaigns, but Jack told me he was ready to leave Connecticut and return to DC. Thankfully, I met Alex, a seasoned aide whose previous boss had recently retired. Just shy of thirty, he sported a neatly trimmed beard and boasted an impressive knowledge of the legislature. While I knew no one in the building, Alex seemed to know everyone: who to call to help me move into my new office, how to order business cards, and which lobbyists were critical to keep on our side. Already, constituents were calling me to ask for help resolving an issue at the DMV or some other state agency. Alex knew which extensions to dial to resolve these issues, too. He took over my schedule and clued me in on how a state senator should spend their time. Although Jack had controlled my calendar on the campaign trail, he and I had lived together for five years. Alex and I had never shared a bunk bed, and I was a little embarrassed about what he might find: e.g., "Buy Katie a Birthday Present," among other reminders I shouldn't need in my calendar.

Alex and I were opposites in just about every way you can imagine. His desk was sparse but included a neat stack of mail and a photo of his golden retriever, Otis. In a matter of days, my desk was buried in a mountain of paperwork that I probably would never need again. Alex packed a healthy, homemade lunch every day. I either skipped lunch or scarfed down a bacon cheeseburger during a meeting. He was paid about double what I was making, and that seemed about right.

Alex scheduled one-on-ones for me with the first selectmen in my district to learn about the top priorities for each town. Then came funding requests from various groups in the community, like parents of children with disabilities, retired teachers, the local YMCA, Alzheimer's Association advocates, unions, and countless other organizations. Once the in-district meetings were done, Alex started to schedule jam-packed days of speed dating with key figures in the capitol building. It was a relatively small cast of characters, since many lobbyists represented more than a dozen groups. For example, one lobbyist might represent Coca-Cola, the Dance Teachers' Club of CT, and the Humane Society. The point of these meetings wasn't to delve into any particular issue but instead to develop a rapport. I could tell that many lobbyists smelled blood, assuming my youth meant I'd be pliable to their clients. Each meeting would last about twenty minutes, and Alex could fit eight or ten of them into a day.

Pretty quickly, we became a strong team. I respected how much he knew about the process that I didn't, and he respected that I wanted to do things just a little bit differently. He sensed when to rescue me from a meeting that dragged on too long, and I did my best not to bother him outside of working hours. Back home, constituents started to approach me at the grocery store and tell me how kind Alex had been while resolving a problem for them.

Alex also taught me some of the benefits of being a state senator. He ordered fancy Senate stationery, explaining that I should be sending letters out to my community. Nearly every morning, I sent him screenshots of local news stories featuring town employees who were retiring or students who made the honor roll. As I arrived at the capitol and walked into a string of meetings, he handed me a stack of congratulatory notes that I could sign when I found a moment.

When the swearing-in ceremony finally arrived, every senator was called on to say a few words. I wanted my first remarks on the floor to help my colleagues (and maybe myself) understand why I was sitting in this seat. But of course, that morning was filled with a million distractions. My dad, lovable but disruptive, had used a canvas bag to smuggle bottles of wine into the Senate gallery and proudly delivered them as a present for Jack. Reporters wanted to talk to my family, but Jack wisely steered them toward Katie instead. Boucher showed up wearing all black.

When Senator Looney stood to address the chamber, he said, "In putting on my tie this morning, I realized that this tie is more than three years older than Senator Will Haskell, who is our new senator from the Twenty-Sixth District." This became a bit of a motif for the next few months. Legislators would tell me anytime they were wearing something older than I was, from their shoes to their glasses to their undergarments.

When it was my turn, I started by talking about my mom. She was sitting behind me in the Senate chamber, looking a bit bewildered by the pageantry of the capitol. Mom didn't pay much attention to politics, and it was hardly her lifelong dream that I become a state senator. But she was smiling ear to ear because she could tell that I was happy.

When I was growing up, my mom had prioritized happiness—specifically my happiness—above all else. There were no rules in our household, and we ate dessert before dinner just as often as we did the other way around. I never had a bedtime, despite Meem's concern that I'd never grow taller if I didn't learn to fall asleep before midnight. But in matters professional and personal, Mom was her own boss. Because she worked so hard, she was determined to enjoy the rare moments when she was off the clock.

Unintentionally, Mom had prepared me for the fast pace of this new job. She doesn't know how to sit still, and she's never lived by a routine in her entire life. Growing up, we spent every night visiting a circuit of friends or family who lived nearby. She didn't care about my report card, or any of the typical parent stuff. When I woke up on the day of the SAT and grumbled that I didn't feel like taking it, she suggested we go get pancakes instead. Now, on the opening day of the session, she was no more or less proud than she had been when I played the third-tree-from-the-left in a high school musical. So long as I was happy, my mom was happy. And her beaming smile gave me the confidence to tell my colleagues why I had run for this seat in the first place.

"I want to recognize somebody who isn't here today. It's somebody who isn't watching on television or isn't waiting to see what happens in the upcoming legislative session. I'm talking about those who avoid politics, who abdicate their role in the policy-making process, who don't think that they could or should vote . . . let alone run for office. In the months ahead, I hope it will be the job of this chamber to reach out to those who are apathetic or pessimistic or too often overlooked. Let's demonstrate the government is a place to come together, and politics, if practiced responsibly, is simply the mission of helping people."

I wanted my colleagues to know that I understood I didn't have decades of experience—but that was the point. At some point in our lives, everyone feels overlooked by the political process. My campaign had brought new voices into the fold, and I was determined to keep doing so now that I was in the Senate. With all of the cameras pointed our way at the capitol that morning, it seemed easy for elected officials to lose sight of the fact that many of our constituents didn't even know Connecticut had a state Senate. I added, "Let's make it our job to encourage others to make that leap of faith, to believe in the good of government, and understand that we need their voice in order to build a better future for Connecticut."

At the governor's inaugural ball that night, Jack, Katie, and I didn't exactly fit in among the wheelers and dealers in tuxedos and gowns. We stood by the bar and watched the newly inaugurated governor dance like Elaine from *Seinfeld*. Maybe he wouldn't fit in perfectly either. Maybe we could work together.

19

Drinking from a Fire Hose

When orientation came to an end, it was time to finally get to work. But what exactly did that mean? Senator Looney had appointed me Senate chair of the Higher Education and Employment Advancement Committee. Unlike the U.S. Congress, Connecticut's legislature includes both senators and representatives on a single committee, meaning each committee has both a House chair and a Senate chair. Representative Gregg Haddad was the House chair of Higher Ed, and he had been working on the college affordability issue since he came to the building as a legislative aide two decades ago. His district included the University of Connecticut, so most of his constituents were younger than I was. He was patient with my basic questions about the legislative process, and shared a desire to improve our community colleges. We instantly made a good team.

Senator Looney also appointed me vice chair of the Government Administration and Elections (GAE), where I had an opportunity to be Mae's right-hand man. This committee provided me a chance to fight for voting rights, something I had talked about often as I went door to door. Additionally, I was assigned to the Transportation, Judiciary, and Environment committees. Although I had worried that I might simply inherit Boucher's committees, assignments are doled out anew by the Senate leadership every two years through an opaque process of policy expertise and political patronage. I felt like these five committees offered an opportunity to deliver for my district and focus on the issues that interested me.

We were fast approaching the deadline to introduce bills, but I still couldn't figure out my password for the legislator portal. Without access to the online system, I scrawled my first few bill requests on a paper form. More seasoned legislators promised that I'd have time to revise the content of the bills later in the committee process, and the most important thing was introducing a bill with the right title. Take, for example, *An Act Concerning Wireless Internet Availability on the New Haven Line of the Metro-North Commuter Railroad.* The title of the bill was about as long as its substance. It read, "Be it enacted by the Senate and House of Representatives in General Assembly convened: That the general statutes be amended to require that wireless Internet accessibility be provided on the New Haven line of the Metro-North Commuter Railroad." This bill would probably never pass, but introducing it was an important part of the process. Later on during the session, I could try to get Wi-Fi on Metro-North included in what's called an "aircraft carrier" bill that passes out of the Transportation Committee. My short and sweet bill would signal to the Department of Transportation and to the leaders on the Transportation Committee that I wanted to start a conversation on the topic.

On small issues and big issues alike, I felt a huge responsibility to deliver on the promises I'd made to the people who elected me. Plus, voters had given us a Democratic trifecta. In other words, our party controlled the governorship and both chambers of the state legislature. There are thirty-six trifectas across the country, with twenty-one held by Republicans. While conservative donors have spent the last decade investing heavily in state legislatures, Democrats have focused on national campaigns (to varying success). From 2010 to 2018, Democrats lost 958 seats in state legislatures across the country, and even in 2018 Republicans outspent us five to one in state legislative races.

Thanks to groups like Run for Something and the Democratic Legislative Campaign Committee, the Left has started to shift meaningful investments to the state level, spurred by the realization that state governments decide countless aspects of our everyday lives, and progressive ideas could be tested in these "laboratories of democracy." We were one of a few Democratic trifectas, so while Washington talked about problems, we could actually solve them. That is, if we could get our acts together.

When Republicans secure a trifecta, they often pass abortion bans and Medicaid work requirements. Democratic trifectas typically legalize cannabis or promote LGBTQ equality. How were we going to use ours? Everybody had a different idea, and it was hard to keep up. Helpfully, all public meetings are broadcast via CT-N, Connecticut's version of C-SPAN. Thanks to hardworking but invisible producers who control the cameras remotely in every room, my colleagues taught me to master the art of being in two or three places at once.

As I voted on banning pesticides in the Environment Committee, I'd watch CT-N on my phone and track the tolls drama unfolding in the Transportation Committee. Meanwhile, I'd use my laptop to watch the debate on a bill in GAE that would end prison gerrymandering. So long as a bill was bipartisan, it wasn't a big deal if you were tied up elsewhere when the votes were called. You could always check in with the committee clerk later on to tell them whether you'd like to vote yea or nay. But if the chair of the committee was concerned that amendments might be called, you'd better be in the room and ready to vote. On amendments, votes can be cast only by those who are actually in the room. Too many absences on one side of the aisle, or even an extended bathroom break by one of your colleagues, can sink a bill.

Much to my frustration, it wasn't rare for multiple committees to take up controversial bills at the exact same time. Alex Kasser and I both served on the Transportation Committee, where we were fighting to fund infrastructure improvements, and the Judiciary Committee, where we were fighting for stricter gun regulations. Unfortunately, the committees were tackling those issues on the same afternoon. So we ran between committee rooms, relying on aides and colleagues to fill us in on which amendment we were actually voting on when we arrived. The most substantive meetings, called "screenings," involved top Democrats and top Republicans on a committee sitting down behind closed doors to decide which bills would move forward. But these negotiations were always made longer by the fact that someone had to race out of the room to vote in another committee.

Being in the capitol reminded me of being in school, except some dysfunctional software had decided to schedule us for classes that met at the same time. The most valuable gossip was shared in the hallways, and we were all eager to maintain a perfect attendance record— something we could brag about to our constituents when report cards came out at the end of the session. The hearings themselves were essentially crash courses in hundreds of topics, with experts and advocates working quickly to bring policy makers up to speed.

In one committee, I learned that donor breast milk isn't covered by Medicaid, and it can cost up to $4 or $5 per ounce. Parents who can't afford this milk risk losing their newborn in the event of a premature birth—a danger that disproportionately impacts low-income families and families of color. The problem, according to Connecticut's commissioner of social services, is that donor breast milk is considered nutrition and not medication. Therefore, it was not categorized as a medical necessity for families in need. Mothers who had lost their children packed the hearing room to fight for a new law expanding Medicaid to include breast milk.

In another committee, I learned that Connecticut ranks forty-ninth when it comes to the affordability of prison phone calls. Perhaps relatedly, our recidivism rate is so high that 60 percent of inmates who were released in 2014 were rearrested within three years of leaving prison. One method of reducing recidivism is allowing incarcerated people to stay in close touch with their loved ones. That way, after serving their time, they have a network to lean on. Unfortunately, Connecticut contracted with a private telecommunications company that made frequent communication unaffordable for most families. Studiously taking notes, I learned that a fifteen-minute phone call could cost up to $4.88 in Connecticut. In New York, that same call would cost only 65 cents. Families often bore the brunt of these costs, and many simply couldn't afford to keep in touch with their fathers, sisters, sons, or other family members behind bars. This was an especially cruel but often overlooked feature of our penal system.

As we raced through the halls between meetings, I vented to Alex that I wanted more time to dig into these issues. If I lingered in a hearing to learn more about breast milk, I'd miss the conversation about prison phone calls. How many good ideas and necessary reforms would fall through the cracks because legislators are always trying to be in multiple places at once? If lawmakers were preoccupied trying to maintain perfect attendance, who was actually doing the work around here?

On one of my first visits to the cafeteria, I asked the woman in line ahead of me what she was planning to order. I already had my eye on the bacon cheeseburger, but months of campaigning had instilled in me a need to chat with strangers.

This woman was Black, looked roughly forty, and had enough wear and tear on her ID badge that I could tell she'd worked in this building for a while.

"You new here?" she asked.

I nodded.

"You'll move up quickly," she said in a way that was both friendly and grim. "White boys always do."

While we waited for our food, she told me that she'd been stuck answering phones for longer than she cared to admit. Unexpectedly frank, she informed me that she had been repeatedly passed over for a promotion. Although I'd been too self-absorbed with my attendance record to take much notice, it wasn't hard to see that nearly everyone who called the shots in this building looked like me. From the legislative leaders (all of whom were white, only one of whom was a woman) to the senior staff, a predominantly white legislature relied on many people of color to actually run the capitol. After that conversation, I started to see how many Black staffers whispered answers into the ears of white legislators who took center stage at a press conference. I noticed how many women were working in the cafeteria, serving food to predominantly male legislators and lobbyists. I realized that the bills I "wrote" were actually drafted by talented female attorneys whose names wouldn't appear in the press.

I've spent a lot of time since 2018 encouraging other people to run for office, promising that launching a campaign is "easier than you expect." But that encouragement, based on my experience, fails to address the unspoken truth that voters were quicker to grant me the benefit of the doubt because I am a white man. In reality, plenty of first-time candidates will find that their campaigns are actually harder than expected, due to xenophobia, racism, and sexism among voters. How many country-club types had supported me during the campaign because I looked like their son or grandson? How many votes had I won by accepting invitations to various men's clubs—invitations I don't believe were often extended to my female colleagues?

One older man actually said that quiet part out loud. He gave me a firm handshake and promised to vote for me at his precinct: New Canaan High School. I thanked him but informed him that people who voted at that precinct were actually in the Thirty-Sixth Senate District. I encouraged him to vote for my friend, Alex Kasser. He looked puzzled, and firmly said, "No chicks," before walking away.

I believe that I owe my unexpected victory to a combination of hard work, good timing, and a talented campaign team. But I cannot ignore the privilege that I was afforded by my identity. How many afternoons had I spent knocking on doors alone, practicing a speech quietly to myself as I made my way between houses? My friend Stephanie Thomas, a candidate for state representative, never ventured out to knock on doors by herself. As a Black woman, she didn't feel safe meandering onto some else's property unannounced.

By the end of my first month at the capitol, my feelings of inadequacy—the paranoia that I couldn't land the plane—didn't go away but instead changed shape. I no longer felt that I wasn't up to the job of being a state senator. Instead, I wondered if it was possible for anyone to do this job in a truly substantive and responsible way. No one could read every bill that came across their desk or sit through every public hearing. The more I learned about the system, the more I worried that well-meaning dilettantes called the shots in this building rather than experts and impacted communities who knew these issues inside and out. Who was I to vote on whether or not prison phone calls should be free, or breast milk should be available to new parents? Of course, I supported these reforms, but I felt embarrassed that the experts had to ask for my support. I wanted not only to be an active listener in the legislature but also to elevate the voices of advocates and activists who didn't have a chance to serve in the Senate.

20

100,000 First Bosses

When I was a student in the Westport public schools, we never took field trips to Hartford or bothered to learn much about the state government. We visited museums in Manhattan, toured the Statue of Liberty, and felt more connected to the city in which so many local parents worked every day. While much of Connecticut roots for the Red Sox and the Patriots, my neighborhood cheered on the Yankees and the Giants. When we saw political ads on television, they touted or maligned New York politicians. Even the mail we sent went through a processing center across the border. When I spoke about the governor in my district, I occasionally had to clarify that I wasn't talking about the one in Albany.

But every once in a while, students from our area did visit the capitol. Whenever they arrived, I would drop everything so that I could tour them around the Senate chamber. I recited the facts that I'd learned from Ms. Ellaneous and asked how they'd vote on various issues I was considering that day. I especially enjoyed asking them who they thought my boss was. Students often guessed the governor or the president of the United States. They were always shocked to find out that my bosses were in fact them. This caused some laughter, but I explained that I worked for each of them, as it was my job to represent their collective view in the Senate.

Keeping in touch with my 100,000 constituents was another source of stress as I learned the ropes in Hartford. Every voter will tell you that they want a legislator who gets stuff done. But what most of them really want is a legislator who is accessible and omnipresent in the district. Being an effective legislator and spending time in the district aren't necessarily complementary goals—in fact, they can work against each other. A few months after I was sworn in, an elderly lady made this clear on Ridgefield's Main Street.

"Where have you been?" she asked. "You used to be in Ridgefield all the time. I never see you anymore."

"I've been in Hartford," I explained. Proud of the work I was doing, I told her about some of the bills that I had proposed.

"We didn't elect you to spend time in Hartford," she scoffed. "We want to see you here in Ridgefield."

The feedback was more than a little confusing. I had thought that my job was to fight for my constituents at the capitol. After all, that's where my office was located. But people lead busy lives, and even if they followed politics in Washington, DC, they didn't have time to follow legislative mechanics at the state level. In their eyes, doing my job meant shaking hands in the grocery store or hosting coffee hours.

Luckily, I had Lauren Meyer and Joe O'Leary to help maintain a presence back home. Lauren, who also commuted from Fairfield County to Hartford every day, was in charge of my "outreach." My age but a thousand times more organized, she was the sort of person I would have texted in college to find out which textbook we were supposed to buy and when the final exam was scheduled. "Outreach" was a catchall term that covered town hall meetings, classroom visits, roundtables, and basically anything that happened outside of Hartford. Lauren was unfailingly polite, but I learned that her sunny demeanor disguised a skill at navigating local politics with sharp elbows. She was exactly who I wanted in my corner when a town hall crowd became unruly or an angry constituent followed me out into the parking lot. Determined to get reelected and frustrated by the amount of time I was spending in Hartford, I worked with Lauren to organize a constant stream of events on the weekends and in the evenings. She was a critical part of the team, especially when the only people who showed up to the weekly coffee hours she organized were anti-vaxxers.

Joe O'Leary was assigned to be my press aide, and he was also new to the building. He'd previously worked for a local newspaper in Connecticut but had jumped at the opportunity to help Democratic lawmakers fight for affordable health care and human rights. Joe cared deeply about the issues, even more than some lawmakers did. Every day, he cranked out press releases and op-eds to place in the local papers back home.

Just a few weeks into the job, my relationships with other lawmakers were already becoming complicated by policy differences and political disagreements. So I found refuge hanging out in cubicles with legislative aides. After all, they were mostly my age and much more willing to laugh about the absurdity of this place. We'd watch CT-N from some hideaway in the capitol and trade stories about unusual constituents. One evening, they brought me to their favorite bar—a grungy watering hole across the street, tucked into the dungeon of the state's armory. Bud Lights were served in plastic cups and the floor had that sticky texture that made it smell like college. The difference in our roles could be awkward, if not for them then at least for me. When a few of the aides invited me to a party at their place after work, I wondered whether it was appropriate for a state senator to hang out with staff members. I decided to go, and we shared pizza, spiked seltzer, and gossip. It was the most relaxed I'd felt in months.

What separated us, though, was how scared I was to lose my job. A term in the state Senate lasts only two years, so I had no choice but to worry about reelection every day. I'd resolved that I wouldn't spend a lifetime in the legislature, but I did want to run again, and I wanted to win. If I didn't, many would chalk up my brief tenure in the Senate as a fluke, or a momentary lapse in judgment by the voters in my district. Maybe it would even discourage other young people from running for office. In order to prove I was up to this job, I needed to make sure I wasn't fired in 2020.

In my early months as a newly elected senator, I focused on reaching out proactively to constituents through public meetings, press releases, and even the occasional robocall. Eventually, I learned that the most effective way to secure reelection was to ensure that the constituents who reached out to me had a positive experience. The truth of the matter is, most people don't necessarily want to think about their state senator very often. When they do, they are probably exceptionally passionate about a bill. When constituents arrived in Hartford to testify at a public hearing, I welcomed them into my office—even if they were there to lobby against a bill I had cosponsored. That included one constituent from Wilton who had taken the day off from work to speak out against legislation that would regulate crisis pregnancy centers. Some of these centers put out false ads, claiming to offer the full spectrum of reproductive health care when in fact they pressure women not to have an abortion. Imagine having strep throat and going to a local clinic, only to find out that they simply pretend to offer antibiotics. Access to reproductive health care can already be expensive and inconvenient—if we can't yet provide comprehensive and affordable health care for all, we should at least prevent faux doctors from setting up trapdoors on the way to meaningful care.

This constituent didn't see it that way. He believed crisis pregnancy centers had a right to engage in deceptive advertising, thanks to the First Amendment. Clearly, we weren't going to change each other's minds. But I heard him out nonetheless and told him that I appreciated his advocacy, even if he wouldn't end up appreciating my vote on the matter.

Most constituents who were passionate about an issue didn't bother driving all the way to Hartford. Instead, they sent emails asking me to vote one way or another. And while I had never reached out to my state senator before, I found that hundreds of people sent this sort of email each week.

I tried to respond to every message I received. Although I didn't always live up to the goal, I'd spend an hour or two before bed firing away replies and prioritizing the constituents who didn't agree with me. That way, they could call me a communist, scum-of-the-earth carpetbagger who lacked the real-world experience necessary to be a state senator, but they couldn't accuse me of being unresponsive.

Most of the time, I didn't lose any sleep over the angry emails. So long as they weren't threatening, I laughed them off. When Gregg Haddad and I introduced a bill to change the fact that diaper-changing tables were only in women's restrooms, one constituent photoshopped my head onto a baby with a full diaper. My friends from college loved it. Katie's favorite nasty comment read: "Hey Willy Boy, I know that you are single. Why in the world would ANY woman want to date you?! Not only are you unattractive, but you oppress the people of CT and you are a pathetic coward!!"

The messages I didn't laugh about, though, were those that blamed me for the very problems I was trying to solve. When constituents complained to me about "decades of fiscal mismanagement," I wanted to remind them that my parents hadn't even met when state lawmakers made expensive promises to state employees. I was as frustrated as they were that generations of policy makers had declined to pay down state bills, let alone save for the future. That sort of neglect of future generations was exactly why I ran for office in the first place.

When constituents wrote to me in all caps to express how much they disliked a clean-energy initiative that might increase the price of gasoline, I wanted to ask how they thought I felt. No one likes paying more to fill up their tank, but the policy makers who came before me had spent their careers avoiding hard decisions and ignoring the science of climate change. Since our parents' and grandparents' generations had done almost nothing to support the transition to clean energy, young people were left with admittedly crappy choices.

Reading through my inbox, I felt like a member of the clean-up crew being blamed for the mess.

Surely every generation resents the problems they've inherited, but I felt as though we'd been dealt a particularly terrible hand. Bruce Gibney's book *A Generation of Sociopaths* paints an overly harsh but intriguing portrait of baby boomers and the chaos they will leave behind. In Washington, lawmakers from this generation spent decades cutting their own taxes while exploding the national debt. They ran for president promising the short-term protection of entitlement programs without ensuring the long-term sustainability of Social Security or Medicaid. They observed countless moments of silence without seriously entertaining stricter gun regulations. And they declined to make long-term investments in infrastructure, conveniently forgetting the fact that infrastructure spending had paved the way for the postwar economic prosperity they enjoyed. Every generation inherits an imperfect world and must fight its own battles, but it drove me nuts that some of the constituents who had gotten us into this mess now resented me for trying to help get us out of it.

However, I knew that passing the buck back to the prior generation wasn't any more productive than passing the buck on to the next generation. So I left any frustrated retorts in my drafts folder and instead started each reply with a sometimes insincere "Thank you," typed with curled toes and clenched teeth.

In contrast, the emails that I most welcomed came from constituents who requested help solving a problem. Providing such a service was, after all, the purpose of government. Unable to reach a live person within the state bureaucracy, these constituents needed to find the right DMV form, resolve a misunderstanding with the tax collector, or ask a question about their unemployment application. With Alex's help, it was my job to be their advocate within the state on issues big and small. The average citizen may not be able to hold a faceless bureaucrat's feet to the fire, but they can certainly hold their elected officials accountable.

Some constituents hadn't exactly warmed up to the idea of asking a twenty-two-year-old for assistance. A few decided to forgo the indignity of reaching out directly and contacted my parents instead. Despite these occasional slights, hearing requests from my community reminded me that writing laws was only part of being a state senator. When my bills got tangled up in a partisan logjam, helping constituents avoid eviction, install a crosswalk, or apply for health insurance felt like a worthwhile endeavor.

One day, we received an email from a constituent who was devastated that her daughter, a young woman with disabilities, had recently been denied funding for a residential assistance program by Connecticut's Department of Developmental Services. We reached out to the department to plead the family's case, and pretty soon they reversed their decision. This long-term housing opportunity provided the parents with the peace of mind that their daughter would receive compassionate and professional care, moving toward a semi-independent life even after they were gone. They called the decision "life-changing," and Alex and I felt gratified to have helped make a meaningful difference.

We worked diligently to resolve everything from routine concerns, such as helping people apply for fishing permits and ensuring that local potholes were filled, to some truly odd dilemmas. I spent months trying to convince the Connecticut Department of Agriculture to intervene in Redding, where more than fifty goats were wreaking havoc on a neighborhood. The goats lacked shelter and water, and some of them had escaped their owner's property and been struck by cars. The owner was unquestionably in violation of a local ordinance regarding how many livestock she could have, but the small town of Redding had no capacity to enforce the law. After months of shuttling between the town and state, the Department eventually seized the goats and transported them to Connecticut's women's prison, where the state operated a farm for rescued animals.

Still, Alex and I faced plenty of problems we couldn't help to solve. A few weeks into my new job, a constituent called repeatedly to complain about the late-night jackhammering related to the highway construction behind his house. He was understandably frustrated by the late-night noise, so I called the site manager on the project to work out an adjustment to the blast schedule. I also visited his house to meet with his neighbors and hear about how it had disrupted their sleep. He wanted me to call off the project altogether—something that was simply not possible. If I didn't return his call immediately, he got mad.

"Let me give you a little private sector advice," he said. "I never leave the office without returning every single call."

Admittedly, I don't have any private sector experience. But I have to imagine that most people don't answer to 100,000 bosses. On the campaign trail, I'd treated every interaction with a voter as though it were a job interview. Now that I had the job, I needed to learn when to stand up for myself and when to accept criticism. Eventually, I figured out how not to take no for an answer, and also when to tell a constituent that I had done all I could do to help.

Even in its architectural design, the legislature is inward facing. When rushing from meeting to meeting, it's easy to get swept up in the notion that people are watching from home, waiting with bated breath to see how you'll vote on every bill and amendment. The reality is that most people aren't. Those who do tune in to the public-access channel will join my grandparents and perhaps a handful of others in watching legislators perform to an imagined audience of thousands. Political theatrics may be a part of the process, but the best way to show your community that you're working hard for them is . . . to actually work hard for them. When the simultaneous meetings had ended and the bills had either passed or been passed over, I found that most people who approached me around town wanted to thank me for helping them fix an issue in their lives. Or better yet, they had heard that I'd helped their neighbor, and they wanted some assistance as well. Hearing feedback on my work from a few of my constituents would always remind me that I had a job to do, much like any other.

21

A Democratic Trifecta . . . Now What?

By April, I had figured out that the most epic fights under the capitol dome occur not between Democrats and Republicans but between Senate Democrats and House Democrats. No clear ideological difference divides the chambers, but rather an age-old game of chicken is played every year. The House will often refuse to take up a controversial item unless the Senate does so first, or vice versa. Neither the Speaker of the House nor the Senate president wants to ask their members to take a tough vote if the other chamber won't also vote on the bill. In other words, we're willing to make hard choices—but only if it accomplishes something.

Coming into the legislature with lofty ambitions and limited know-how, I was astounded by how many good ideas were dying because of this sort of legislative gamesmanship. Take tolls, for example. Connecticut is the only state on the East Coast that doesn't have tolls. This means that we pay for road repaving, bridge renovations, and other infrastructure upgrades by ourselves, rather than asking out-of-state drivers and trucking companies passing through Connecticut to chip in. Governor Lamont thought that our lack of tolls made no sense, and I agreed. Situated between Boston and New York, Connecticut was a major artery for truckers and travelers.

Although they paid some modest gas taxes, these paled in comparison to the sums paid via tolls to our neighboring states. Why should we allow them to wear down our roads and clog our highways without paying for the upkeep? With our transportation fund approaching insolvency, we couldn't afford to be so generous. Without tolls, Connecticut was rapidly approaching the day when we could no longer afford to fill potholes, let alone speed up the trains.

I supported efforts to develop a twenty-first-century tolling system that provided a discount to Connecticut residents and commuters. Most importantly, it would make life better for the residents of Fairfield County by funding long-overdue projects.

But the Republicans had issued a warning to those who served in the legislature: "Vote for Tolls, Lose at the Polls." They organized a road show, traveling to towns across Connecticut and whipping up outrage about our proposal. Now that the bill had passed out of committee, it was stuck in legislative limbo.

Despite the growing public pressure, I believed there were enough Democrats in the Senate willing to push tolls over the finish line. The Speaker of the House claimed to have just enough votes to pass the proposal. But neither chamber wanted to go first, for fear that the other chamber would chicken out. It was impossible to get a precise vote count, since no legislator wanted to be on the record in support of tolls unless they had to be. At one point, the top leaders considered exchanging letters disclosing their respective "yes" votes. If one chamber reneged on the deal and tabled the bill, the list would be made public.

With our efforts on tolls stalled, I decided to double down on another major priority: college affordability. As the chair of the Higher Education Committee and the youngest member of the General Assembly, I felt responsible for making sure that the next generation of students could afford to pursue a degree of their choosing. I had been lucky enough to graduate from Georgetown without a cloud of debt hanging over my head, but most grads across the country weren't so fortunate. College tuition at both public and private institutions had exploded, and student loans now exceeded credit card bills or auto loans when it came to household debt. While boomers were able to work their way through college, the average cost of a four-year degree had risen from $26,902 in 1989 ($52,982, adjusted for inflation) to $104,480 in 2016. Some will grumble that wages also rose during that same period, and they're right. The problem is that tuition costs increased nearly eight times more than wages did.

Gregg, the House chair of the Higher Ed Committee, and I set our sights on making Connecticut's colleges more affordable. And while we didn't have the ability to tell private institutions to lower their tuition, we could rein in the rising costs of attending community college. While residents in 2002 might have paid $1,888 for a year's worth of tuition and fees, by 2019 the cost had more than doubled to $4,476. Not coincidentally, student enrollment at community colleges was declining. When I took office, state officials told me to expect a 2.5 to 3 percent enrollment decline among full-time community college students in 2019. The actual decline amounted to 4.7 percent, with five campuses experiencing a decline of more than 5 percent. This was in line with a trend across public and private institutions: fewer students were pursuing higher education. Between 2012 and 2019, college enrollment in Connecticut declined by 6.5 percent, dropping from nearly 197,000 students to 183,981.

In 2012, former senator Rick Santorum made headlines for calling President Obama "a snob" since he wanted "everybody in America to go to college." He was playing to a Tea Party crowd in Michigan, pushing back against the Obama administration's efforts to make college more affordable. These efforts were, at least in part, driven by the belief that students should have an opportunity to choose their own path rather than see their options decided by the size of their parents' bank accounts. But they were also driven by an economic reality: twenty-first-century jobs increasingly required some amount of higher education. In Connecticut, we know that, by 2025, 70 percent of jobs will require a degree beyond a high school diploma. Unfortunately, we are nowhere close to meeting that demand. Recently, we've been moving in the opposite direction. Gregg and I wanted to reverse the decline in enrollment and produce 300,000 more graduates.

Connecticut is lucky to have exceptional private institutions, including Yale, Wesleyan, Connecticut College, and many more. Yet, across all campuses, only 38 percent of students who earned their degree in Connecticut stayed in the state to join the workforce. This statistic was pretty abysmal, bringing us to a national ranking of 37th for graduate retention. But public colleges, and specifically community colleges, provided a bright spot in an otherwise bleak picture. Within nine months of graduation, 76 percent of public college graduates were working in Connecticut. And as an added benefit, reducing the cost of community college fostered greater competition in the marketplace. If the tuition gap between community college and private institutions grew large enough, private schools might start to lose students and feel pressure to drop their tuition.

Gregg and I looked to other states for proven solutions. When Democrats had achieved a trifecta in Washington, Oregon, California, Nevada, Hawaii, Delaware, New Jersey, New York, and Rhode Island, they had decided to provide free community college for at least two years. We wanted Connecticut to be next.

Although we braced ourselves for the price tag, we soon learned that passing a debt-free community college program wouldn't be all that expensive. The Office of Fiscal Analysis (a group of smart, apolitical number crunchers who sit on the fifth floor of the Legislative Office Building) determined that eliminating tuition payments would cost less than $6 million a year. You read that correctly: Giving every high school graduate in Connecticut who had never gone to college the chance to earn a two-year degree for free would cost about the same amount we spent on purchasing and maintaining the state police fleet each year. For context, that's less than 1/15th of 1 percent of Connecticut's budget. What amounts to a rounding error could make a world of difference for young people across the state.

In fact, fiscal analysts predicted that our community colleges would *make* money by eliminating tuition. While that may seem counterintuitive, the promise of free community college typically inspires more students to apply. Since our program would require all applicants to fill out the Free Application for Federal Student Aid (FAFSA), many young people who wouldn't have otherwise applied would learn that they qualified for financial assistance in the form of Pell grants. Our twelve community colleges would end up seeing more students *and* more federal dollars.

When I knocked on doors, many voters griped to me that we live in a donor state. That means Connecticut residents pay more in federal taxes than we receive in return from the federal government. In concrete terms, we only get 74 cents back for every dollar we send to Washington, DC. (For context, Mississippi receives $2.13 in return for every dollar they pay in federal taxes.) Making community college free, and encouraging more students to complete the FAFSA along the way, would provide a chance for Connecticut to bring back more federal assistance for families who would invest the money into higher education.

Gregg and I worked hard to pass our bill out of committee, but in order to become law it needed the strong support of at least one chamber. Senator Flexer taught me how to advocate for the program in our caucus room, and thankfully, my Democratic colleagues in the Senate were on board. Once the bill had passed in the Higher Ed Committee, Senator Cathy Osten fought in the Appropriations Committee to secure the necessary funding.

Throughout the process, Republicans tried to undermine the idea and warned about the supposed danger of giving away anything for free. During our meetings, they raised objections that students who didn't pay tuition wouldn't have skin in the game, and therefore wouldn't do well in school. I pointed out that even without paying tuition, community college students had plenty of skin in the game. Attending college full-time often required sacrificing work opportunities, paying for childcare, and investing in the cost of books or transportation. They'd roll their eyes and say that they hadn't needed a handout when they were in school. Gregg and I brought charts to show that declining public investments in higher education had led the cost of earning a degree to skyrocket beyond anything they could have imagined paying in the twentieth century.

But arguments with the Republicans, whether in committee or on the floor of the Senate, were just for show. The real fight transpired behind the scenes with other Democrats. More moderate members of our party wanted to impose a means test, or a household income limit, on the program. Gregg and I hated that idea. Having closely studied this policy in other states, we knew that adding conditions to the promise of free college would overcomplicate the message and undercut a potential increase in enrollment. Just across the border, New York had passed a complex means-tested free college program that failed to inspire a significant enrollment increase. Meanwhile, across our other border, Rhode Island's universal program sparked a 47 percent increase in enrollment in its second year, driven in large part by a boost in students of color. The difference boiled down to one factor: free college is a lot easier to advertise when there are no strings attached.

Still, some fellow Democrats argued that middle-class taxpayers shouldn't foot the bill for millionaires and billionaires who send their kids to community college. Gregg and I countered that millionaires and billionaires typically don't send their kids to community colleges. It would be awesome if they did, as we'd see greater socioeconomic and racial diversity in classrooms across the state and country. But the crux of our case came down to this: as higher education became more necessary, it became a public good. No one argues that Connecticut should impose an income limit on publicly maintained parks, roads, sidewalks, or K–12 schools. No one raises alarms when the sons and daughters of millionaires or billionaires ride a school bus that middle-class taxpayers helped fund. We believed it was time to stop thinking in terms of K–12 and start thinking seriously about how the government could provide a K–14 education for all who were interested.

Throughout these negotiations, we visited nearly every community college in the state to rally support for the program. We heard from young people, both in person and on social media, about how free community college would impact their life. As the bill slowly moved forward, I watched people share the news on Facebook. Some of my favorite reactions:

"Guess nursing school is going to happen sooner than I thought."

"Maybe I'll move back home now."

"I'll definitely go for early childhood development if this is true."

"Opportunity is knocking."

"My turn to learn things."

Their enthusiasm motivated me to keep fighting when I was feeling discouraged about the challenges of lawmaking. I had begun to realize that Democratic trifectas don't provide any guarantees—tolls were seeming less and less likely by the day, and I hadn't yet gotten any of my other priorities across the finish line. But if and when we work out our intraparty differences, trifecta states can serve as critical laboratories to put progressive policies into action. Despite all the news coverage dedicated to battles in the U.S. Congress, successes on the state level may be the best evidence that progressive policies make people's lives better. Dig into the details of average life expectancy, the number of children who live in poverty, or the percentage of people who have health insurance, and you'll find that blue states perform vastly better than red states. We sweat the details in a small state like Connecticut in the hope that policy makers across the country will see that what works here could work everywhere.

22

What *Schoolhouse Rock* Didn't Tell You

Did you know that lobbyists literally sit in the lobby all day? I didn't. Every day, the lobbies and hallways of the capitol are crowded with people who peddle influence and professionalize small talk. Some of them earn more than an entire committee of legislators combined. A few months into the job, I came to realize that everybody in the capitol seemed to know each other. In some cases, they were even related. A consummate capitol insider named Carroll Hughes bent my ear about the importance of protecting small liquor stores that faced unfair competition from the cheaper big-box stores. A few minutes later, his son Josh lobbied me on behalf of those big-box stores. Former Speakers of the House who once wielded the most powerful gavel in the building now sit on benches scattered throughout the building, waiting to catch a lawmaker on his or her way to the bathroom. If the clock is ticking and they really need your vote, they might even follow you into the bathroom.

Once upon a time, lobbyists hosted debauched parties for legislators inside the capitol building. Gross stories about women, drugs, and liquor were whispered to new legislators with a bit too much yearning for the good ole days. Nowadays, thanks to clean government laws and a legislature that isn't *entirely* composed of old men, lobbyists trade on information instead. With so much happening at the capitol, only the lobbyists have the time and resources to track bills and count votes.

Vin taught me that not all lobbyists peddle nefarious special interests. Although being a "lobbyist for good" seemed like an oxymoron when I arrived in Hartford, I learned that there are some lobbyists who fight every day for environmental protections and others who work to end homelessness. These are called "white hat" lobbyists, and they could be crucial allies in gathering information, organizing press conferences, and pressuring colleagues who were on the fence about an upcoming vote. On the other side of the equation, there are "black hat" lobbyists who fight against pesticide regulation, youth smoking restrictions, or puppy mill bans. Most of the folks you find in the lobby fall somewhere in between. These "gray hat" lobbyists have plenty of good clients, and a few bad ones who pay the bills. They might request a meeting to discuss domestic violence interventions, then casually mention the reasons we shouldn't ban fracking waste. Friendly faces who help you whip votes on student loan relief may then try to convince you that exposing the Catholic Church to liability for sexual assault is a bad idea. Believe it or not, even the gray and black hat lobbyists could be useful.

Take the oil and gas industry, for example. Their team quickly defeated a bill I supported to ban gasoline zone pricing, the process by which gas distributors coordinate (you could say collude) to keep prices high in certain zip codes. On my drive to work every day, I see gas prices steadily decline as I travel north. In Westport, drivers can pay almost a dollar more per gallon than drivers in Rocky Hill. I helped organize a bipartisan group of legislators to support a ban on zone pricing and an increase of competition in the marketplace. Oil and gas lobbyists, representing the gas distributors, whipped enough votes to kill our proposal. So we had our disagreements.

But Vin, who relishes unusual alliances, showed me that the enemy of my enemy could be my friend. In the Environment Committee,

I proposed a bill to crack down on leakage in natural gas pipelines. Methane gas, which too often leaks from aging underground pipelines, has a catastrophic effect on the ozone. According to the League of Conservation Voters, methane gas "traps at least thirty times more heat in our atmosphere than carbon dioxide and is the second largest contributor to climate change." While other states tolerated almost no leakage, Connecticut allowed these companies to leak 3 percent of this dangerous gas without facing any repercussions. In 2016, the Sierra Club found that the city of Hartford alone saw 3,000 cubic feet of gas leaked into the atmosphere every day. That added up to 313 metric tons per year.

If those environmental arguments didn't do the trick, I reminded colleagues that our constituents are charged for the leaked gas that they never actually receive. In the eyes of those who sold and distributed home heating oil, this was tremendously unfair. Connecticut doesn't tolerate a single drop of leaked oil, but the amount of leaked gas in Hartford alone equates to 320 gallons of oil spilled onto the road every day. Surely no homeowner would pay a delivery crew who had leaked oil along the road and arrived with a half-empty truck.

Constantly in competition with natural gas companies, the heating oil folks loved my bill. In an unexpected turn of events, we suddenly had powerful oil lobbyists working hand in hand with leading environmentalists. With their help, our bill made it out of committee. In the weeks that followed, I saw similarly odd alliances working toward a common goal in other committees. Private colleges and universities fought to increase funding for student financial aid, but they whipped votes against free community college since it might lure students away from their increasingly expensive campuses. Earthy-crunchy liberals who distrusted pharmaceutical companies stood beside conservative religious zealots to oppose legislation that would require most schoolchildren to be vaccinated. Some Republicans, without a hint of irony, even adopted the slogan, "My body, my choice." The American Civil Liberties Union (ACLU) stood with police unions to oppose a bill that would use speed-enforcement cameras to crack down on speeding near schools and hospitals. The ACLU's skepticism of data collection and the police union's desire not to be replaced by technology brought the unlikely couple together. Strange bedfellows were everywhere in this building, and in Vin's eyes, that keeps our business interesting. After all, you don't have to love every business partner.

As for working across the aisle? With some colleagues, it wasn't hard to find niche areas of mutual interest. Tom O'Dea and I had gotten over our feisty exchange at the Wilton debate and worked together to try and put opioids into blister packages as opposed to the amber vials. That way, doctors and patients could keep track of the medication and make sure that pills don't end up being sold or consumed on the illicit market. Tom was a Republican who showed up to work ready to compromise, understanding that he was in the minority but hoping to eke out a few victories for his district. Some legislators, however, had no interest in cooperating. Instead, they saw government as the enemy. One smiled at me in a meeting and summed it up in shockingly blunt terms: "Will, you came into this building to do something. I came to this building to stop things from being done."

23

Legislating Isn't Rocket Science

I f running for office seems daunting to young people, actually being in office can seem unthinkable. When I talk to college students who want to get involved in politics, too many of them balk when I suggest that they run for office themselves. Sometimes they're worried that they don't have enough knowledge to play a role in creating public policy. They're usually concerned that their colleagues won't respect them. Most are not sure if they'll be all that effective. I was worried about those things, too. But elected officials don't need to be experts in order to have a vision for how their community could be better. Sure, I occasionally stepped out of a meeting to google something in a bathroom stall, then returned pretending that I fully understood the intricacies of the prevailing wage debate. And I visited lots of realtors' offices to talk with them about fluctuating home values and conveyance tax rates, which is a little absurd considering I couldn't yet afford to rent my own apartment. But plenty of legislators have firsthand knowledge about buying a home, or the rise and fall of their 401(k). Not nearly enough of them know how challenging it is to afford rent in Fairfield County.

I hesitated to run for office because I didn't think I had enough experience to be a lawmaker. And skeptical voters I met on the campaign trail reminded me of my inexperience constantly. In fairness to them, my first few months in Hartford confirmed my worst fears—writing laws is unfailingly complicated and endlessly nuanced. Before voting on the teacher pension re-amortization plan, I had to figure out what re-amortization meant. But I rolled up my sleeves, paid attention during public hearings, and read through the expert testimony. Like any job, I eventually got better. I discovered that if I did my homework, I was ready to vote on any bill by the time it reached the Senate floor.

Luckily, I wasn't facing this challenge alone. The twenty-two Democratic senators were a small enough group that we could often act as a team, and our freshman class kept in close touch about upcoming votes. If I worried that a bill was too progressive for my fiscally conservative district, I'd touch base with Senator Needleman, a businessman with decades of experience in the private sector. If I didn't understand the complexities of special education funding, I'd gut check with Senator Abrams, who used to be a special educator herself. If I couldn't understand how a bill would impact workers and workplaces, I'd text Senator Kushner, who knew the labor movement like the back of her hand. Senator Looney had dedicated an unoccupied office near the Senate chamber for our freshman class, and Vin took to calling it the Freshman Dorm. We never got around to putting up angsty posters, but we spent plenty of time in that room trading gossip and insights.

Soon we developed the vocabulary to track the progress of bills as they zigged and zagged through the building. Generally speaking, most bills start when an individual legislator (or a group of legislators) have an idea. For example, State Representative Jane Garibay and I had an idea to address government inefficiency. Both of us new to the building, we got to know each other at freshman orientation and quickly began to strategize together about how to show the swing voters in our district that we intended to put their tax dollars to good use. In Jane's hometown, municipal employees who suggested reforms that would help town hall run more cost-effectively received a modest financial reward. It was a smart idea: enlisting the help of folks who actually work within the government, since they know where to trim the fat better than anyone else. So we proposed a bill to scale up that program for the entire state government, a bureaucracy with roughly 50,000 people. If an employee reported wasteful or duplicative spending, and their report resulted in cost savings for the state the next year, they would receive a small percentage of those savings.

Once a bill is introduced, it's referred to the relevant committee. This one was referred to the Government Administration and Elections Committee. Perhaps recognizing that Jane and I would face a steep reelection soon, Mae agreed to draft the bill, then hold a public hearing. Unlike in Congress, where a select group of experts are invited to testify, Connecticut hearings are open to anyone. Members of the public can submit testimony or speak in front of the committee for three minutes. Not too many people came to testify about our bill, but it attracted plenty of support when it was called for a vote. Even Senator Rob Sampson, dubbed in one profile as the "dissenting senator" who relished voting no on bipartisan bills, supported it. After clearing the committee, it was headed to the full Senate.

There was a lull after the bill passed out of committee and before it reached the floor. Committees toiled away on a few dozen more bills until April, racing to meet various deadlines. Once the chairs had either advanced or killed each bill, the Democrats in the Senate started to meet for lunch on a regular basis. Over heavy Italian meals served in the caucus room, Marty would ask each senator to quickly summarize the bills that had passed through their committee. "Quickly" was more of an aspiration than a hard-and-fast rule, and the lunches lasted hours. These long discussions sometimes brought the rest of the capitol to a halt, and I began to understand why the Senate was hated by the House of Representatives. As Jonathan often reminded me, he saw the House Republicans as the opposition but the Senate Democrats as the enemy.

These lunches ensured that we were never caught off guard when a bill reached the Senate floor. Sadly, there aren't enough hours in the day to read every page of every bill, and on some days we'd vote on dozens of bills in a matter of minutes. "Consent calendars" allowed us to group bills together, meaning we might vote yea on a handful of new laws with the press of a single button.

I learned that the crux of my job was to stay on top of all Higher Ed legislation. Jeanie, the committee clerk who had done this job for decades, placed each of those bills into a folder alongside a summary from nonpartisan analysts, a forecast of what the bill might cost the state, and key pieces of testimony that had been submitted during the hearing. I kept those folders in my Senate desk and meticulously ordered and reordered them by priority, then quietly practiced how I would explain them in the caucus room or on the Senate floor.

Honesty is a crucial component of the process. Within the caucus room, we relied on each other to flag whether or not a bill was controversial (that is, did every member of the committee vote for it?) or politically fraught ("Representative so-and-so campaigned on this, but Senator so-and-so hates it"). These closed-door meetings, open to only a few senior staff members, were uniquely devoid of pageantry. There was no camera to perform to and no vernacular to adopt. We were just talking, asking our friends if they had considered the potential impact that their bill might have on local breweries, or dental hygienists, or whomever.

The purpose of these long caucuses wasn't just to share ideas—Marty, at the head of the table, was always counting toward the critical number of eighteen. The Senate has thirty-six members, meaning eighteen yea votes are necessary to pass each bill. The lieutenant governor, a Democrat, can be called on to break the tie. Since we had twenty-two Democratic senators, up to four could "take a pass" (that means vote no) or "take a walk" (that means skip the vote altogether) on a bill without jeopardizing its passage. If you found four other colleagues who agreed that a bill was a bad idea, you could effectively guarantee it wouldn't receive a vote in the Senate.

When Senator Cathy Osten, a former corrections official who chaired the powerful Appropriations Committee, presented pension contracts that needed to be approved, I moved my shaking hands under the table as I explained to the room that my constituents really wanted to see the state payroll shrink. My district had sent me to Hartford, in part, to vote against contracts like these. Cathy understood, but she wasn't happy. On the other hand, when I pushed for stricter gun regulations, she'd point out that there were more guns in her district than there were people. We both understood that we faced political pressure back home and never disparaged the other in the press. Operating as a team required acknowledging that our districts were vastly different, even if Connecticut was a small state.

Once we had discussed each of the bills in caucus, filed any amendments, and confirmed the eighteen votes necessary for passage, it was time to negotiate with the Republicans. In essence, the Republican strategy was to run out the clock. They knew that any bill we hadn't passed by June 5th would die, so their power grew each day as that deadline drew closer. Our delegation to the Republican caucus room consisted of Vin, the Senate's bad cop, and his deputy, Courtney, the good cop. Courtney had memorized every senator's wish list and knew how to reward good behavior and punish bad behavior. Behind a knowing smile and an affable demeanor, she wielded a vast power. But, politics aside, I genuinely liked her. Every so often, legislative negotiations fell by the wayside and I saw Courtney's genuine passion for an issue like improving mental health on college campuses.

Like kids with a Christmas list, Democratic senators would text Courtney a list of our bills in order of priority. Our hard-fought efforts would become numbers on the sticky note in her hand as she walked across the hall to negotiate with the Republicans. It was critical to get the best bills through the Senate as quickly as possible, giving the House plenty of time to debate and pass them before June

5th. Sometimes, Courtney would text back to ask if we were willing to trade a Republican bill in exchange for shortening the debate on one of our bills.

"Is SB 745 ok for you?"

I flipped through my folders looking for SB 745: *An Act Requiring a Feasibility Study on the Establishment of a Controlled-Environment Agricultural Program at the Regional Community Technical Colleges.* It wasn't a priority for me, but it was important to Senator Heather Somers, a Republican who represents some farms in eastern Connecticut.

"Sure, but only if it means I get HB 6890 today."

HB 6890 was our effort to push back against Betsy DeVos's Title IX rollback and protect survivors of sexual assault on campus. Courtney would return to our caucus room having hashed out the day's agenda: here's what we got, here's what we needed to do in exchange, here's what they're blocking.

Why negotiate with Republicans when Democrats held a sizable majority? We often wondered the same thing while killing time in the Freshman Dorm. The answer comes down to a time-honored tradition of permitting limitless debate on the House and Senate floors. The Republicans knew that any bill Marty allowed to come to the Senate floor had already secured the eighteen votes necessary for passage. However, their members could slow everything down by asking hundreds of questions to the proponent of the bill, or delving into monologues that were just barely related to the substance of the legislation. So when Courtney walked into the Republican caucus room to determine the daily agenda, she wasn't looking for Republican votes. She was negotiating how long they'd fight each item.

My Republican colleagues are not to be underestimated when it comes to stamina. Controversial bills are called "talkers," and those filibusters could last long into the night. The most skilled members of their caucus could seamlessly bounce between old family stories and legislative minutia. The least skilled among them resorted to reading aloud the emails he had received from constituents. The substance of their words didn't really matter, except to the stenographer. The point was to make us all miserable.

Like a bureaucratic fairy tale, our bills risked turning into pumpkins at midnight on the last night of session. If Republicans decided that my bill was a talker on June 4th, I was screwed. In short, talkers needed to be called for a vote early in the spring, since Republican ramblings can last days but not months.

So while Courtney was negotiating what would and wouldn't be a talker, I reviewed Higher Ed bills to figure out which ones were most important. Which should come first: A bill to address the mental health of students or one to tackle food insecurity on campus? If and when either bill was called for a vote, I'd need to defend it on the floor. That required staying up to speed on the bills I cared deeply about, and the ones that made technical changes I only vaguely understood. Senator Tony Hwang, the top Republican (called the ranking member) of the committee, didn't make my job easier. Even if he eventually decided to vote in favor of the bill, he'd pepper me with a dozen or so "clarifying questions." Since I never knew which bills would wind up on Courtney's sticky note, I got into the habit of preparing for everything. For weeks in April, I'd brush up on the arcane regulations concerning the Connecticut Health and Educational Facilities Authority, only to find out that that bill was too much of a talker to bring for a vote anyway.

When my bills finally made the list, I sometimes felt as though my Republican colleagues were just waiting for me to screw up. Any moment now, I'd say something dumb and reveal that I was wholly unqualified for this job. After all, Tony probably knew the answers to just about every question he asked. With a wink and a nudge, he'd explain to the chamber that he was asking these detailed questions for the purpose of "legislative intent." As if passing some words on a page into law wasn't scary enough, legislative intent is something judges will one day look to when they try to interpret the statutes. So that offhand answer I give to the twenty-seventh question lobbed at me could actually decide how the bill is implemented in the real world.

Without any legislative experience under my belt, I lost sleep over potential misstatements on the floor. And in the caucus room, I needed my colleagues to slowly explain what phosphate bywastes were and how they related to anaerobic digesters. But on other days, I found myself taking the lead in explaining issues that impacted my generation. My recent experience as a college student helped me understand the mental health crisis facing young people and the prevalence of sexual misconduct on campus. In the caucus room and in the Freshman Dorm, I discovered that legislators learn from each other and rely on the expertise of friends. Given the breadth of complex issues that wind their way through the capitol building, the authority on Medicaid may be the neophyte on public transit. Taking the time to brush up on an unfamiliar issue was part of the process. As long as I could listen, I could be a legislator.

One day, the cost-savings bill that Jane and I had introduced made it onto Courtney's list. It passed the Senate by a vote of 35-1— Sampson, back to dissenting, now opposed the bill. Thankfully not a talker, it was soon called for a vote in the House of Representatives. Jane was undergoing treatment for breast cancer that day, so I called her from the House floor to let her know that our very first bill was almost across the finish line. Later that week, Governor Lamont signed it into law. We had encountered plenty of stops and starts along the way, and the bill had been improved as it worked its way through committee, then caucus, and then both floors. But passing a law, as it turns out, isn't impossible.

24

Making Friends, Losing Friends

Jack and I had developed a pretty simple formula for email blasts during the campaign. Our "How I'd Vote" emails followed a script: find a bill that Boucher had voted on, explain why her vote was objectionable, and tell people how I would have voted. By criticizing her vote to allow firearms inside state parks, for instance, we showed the community why change was necessary and provided a preview of how I would represent them if given the chance.

By May, however, I was voting on dozens of bills each day, and I winced thinking back to how black and white those emails had been. Like most candidates, I'd adopted campaign rhetoric that embraced moral absolutes. Of course, there were some votes that fit neatly into that binary vision. Voting for the safe storage of guns or the expansion of voting rights was, in my mind, unquestionably the right thing to do. But many more votes fell into a gray area. I learned that being a lawmaker involved less relishing in the righteousness of a particular vote than it did grappling with the potential downsides of every decision.

For example, I wanted Connecticut to be a leader in transitioning to renewable energy, but renewable energy is more expensive than natural gas, and much more expensive than coal. For colleagues who represent less-privileged communities, arguments about the sustainability of our energy grid can be less than convincing when their constituents can't afford to keep the lights on. According to the U.S. Energy Information Administration, one in three American families has trouble paying their energy bills.

As a general rule, energy bills are considered affordable if they stay under 6 percent of a household's total income. Low-income households in Connecticut pay 8–19 percent of their income, on average, toward those bills. Too often, this leads to utility shutoffs that eventually cause homelessness. In short, demands for cleaner energy had to be weighed against their impact on the cost of energy for families who already struggle to pay the bills. Governing requires grappling with both truths at the same time, whereas campaigning didn't.

Becoming more comfortable as a state senator meant learning that I couldn't please everyone, and I made peace with the idea of losing some friends. Many of the moms who had boosted my campaign by hosting cocktail party fundraisers were outraged when I supported the legalization of marijuana. They viewed pot as a gateway drug, and they didn't want their teenagers anywhere near it. When I vented to Governor Lamont about the predicament, he pointed out that most of them had likely passed around a joint once upon a time.

While campaigning alongside groups like Moms Demand Action and Connecticut Against Gun Violence, I bonded with activists who had lost their son or daughter because a firearm was all too accessible. As a member of the Judiciary Committee, I fought alongside them to pass stricter gun laws. But when that same committee considered criminal justice reforms, I found myself at odds with some of those friends.

The Clean Slate Bill, for example, would expunge the criminal records of individuals who had served their time and were not arrested for another offense in the years that followed. The bill aimed to address the numerous hurdles that formerly incarcerated individuals face, from housing to employment to educational opportunities. In Connecticut, 60 percent of people released from prison have yet to find a job one year later. In order to help give these folks a second chance, we wanted to expunge their record and help them avoid a lifetime of discrimination.

But for those who have seen their loved ones harmed, the idea of giving the person responsible a clean slate is excruciating. Over these difficult conversations, I learned to move beyond the campaign-style thinking that every voter was either with me or against me. Now that I was in office, most would fall somewhere in between. If I was drawn to campaigning because I liked being liked, governing would prove I was in the wrong business.

My colleagues taught me that disagreeing with friends was part of the process. When Marty introduced a bill that I couldn't support, I was worried he'd be furious. Before putting out my statement in opposition, I stopped by his office to speak with him about it. To help break the ice, I brought a tie given to me by my friend, State Representative Jason Doucette.

"Marty, I know you mentioned on the opening day of the session that your tie was older than I am," I said. He chuckled again at the joke. "So I wanted to give you a tie older than you are."

Known for his sense of humor, Marty loved it. He understood why I had to oppose his bill—the Twenty-Sixth District had been represented by a Republican during his entire term in the legislature, so he knew I was walking a political tightrope back home. Marty was the most skillful political strategist in the building, and he wanted to make sure I was reelected.

Disagreements about my work in Hartford even found their way into family dinners. Meem's favorite restaurant, located around the corner from their house, was Matsu Sushi. She and Big Bob ate dinner there so often that the staff had given her a nickname, and they knew Big Bob's bento box preference without having to ask. When Meem had accidentally called in an order for 300 California rolls to go instead of 30, they offered her a gift certificate that she used over the course of the year.

One day, the employees of Bridgewater, the hedge fund based in Westport, really did order 300 California rolls, plus a lot of other sushi. The largest hedge fund in the world apparently had a similarly large appetite, and their order was so big that they called it in a few days in advance. Overwhelmed by the request, the owners of Matsu Sushi forced two of their longtime employees, Jianming Jiang and Liguo Ding, to work three consecutive shifts, totaling thirty-six hours. When the employees refused, they were fired—a clear violation of their statutory rights as workers, and just a terrible way to treat people. Even after the National Labor Relations Board demanded that the employees be reinstated and compensated, the restaurant refused.

I met with the workers and, through a translator, heard firsthand about how they were deprived of dignity and respect in the workplace. Although they didn't live in my district, it seemed like my job to represent the people who worked in this community as well. So I agreed to join them on the picket line.

Meem was horrified when she saw photos in the local paper of me protesting outside Matsu Sushi. She reminded me of all the friendly staff members she had come to know. At the five-person picket line, I shook hands with the protesters and addressed a small group of reporters. "Here's my message to the owners," I said. "Listen to the NLRB, reinstate these workers, and I will be the first in line for a table." To residents of Westport, I pleaded that they not break the picket line. "Instead, get to know these remarkable men whose rights were violated. If you work in Westport, you are a part of this town and we care about how you are treated."

Unfortunately, that message carried more weight with Westport diners than it did with the owners. Matsu Sushi soon closed permanently, much to Meem's chagrin. I don't believe Jianming and Liguo ever received their back pay, and many other employees at the restaurant saw their place of employment go dark. I'm not well-schooled in labor activism, but it's not clear to me that right prevailed over wrong in the case of Matsu Sushi.

Nearly every day in Hartford left me questioning whether I had made the right decision and wondering how my voting record would look to those who weren't privy to backroom negotiations. In late May, the Senate deliberated on a bill that extended health care coverage for the treatment of post-traumatic stress to first responders. For years, some of my colleagues had been working to provide this vital assistance to the men and women who run toward a problem when the rest of us run away. In many cases, the tragedies they encounter on the job weigh on them long after a shift ends. Since most conversations about post-traumatic stress center around veterans returning from combat zones, we tend to forget that our neighbors in police, firefighter, and EMS uniforms are struggling, too.

Here's the problem: when Senator Cathy Osten briefed our caucus on the bill, she disclosed that it covered only police officers and firefighters, not EMS workers. Just days before, I'd marched in Memorial Day parades alongside EMS crews, and they had shared stories with me about watching children take their last breath in the back of an ambulance. Some of them had stepped away from the job after responding to the tragedy at Sandy Hook Elementary School.

Cathy had been working on this bill for years, negotiating with municipalities about what level of benefits they could afford to cover and for which employees. This was the best deal she could get, and including EMTs would have killed the compromise. Voting nay wouldn't have been fair to police officers and firefighters who clearly deserve these protections. But voting yea meant letting down the EMS workers in my district.

Cathy needed a final vote count, and her eyes narrowed on me. She hadn't lost the skills required of a corrections officer. This bill mattered to her, and she knew the vote would be close. When I shared my hesitation, she told me I'd be flushing away years of work.

I stepped outside the caucus room and paced around the railing under the gold dome of the capitol. My stomach in knots, I decided to call Mike, a longtime EMS worker in Weston, to explain the predicament. Mike gave me his honest response, as I knew he would. He said excluding EMS workers amounted to a punch in the gut, and he reminded me about some of the horrors he and his colleagues had faced. But when I asked how he would vote if he were in my position, Mike sighed and acknowledged that he'd vote yea. Sometimes, even the people you disappoint recognize that it's your job to do so. Those "How I'd Vote" emails were always sincere, but they were perhaps a bit flippant in ignoring the compelling arguments on both sides of nearly every issue.

As I got better at my job, I found out that nearly every vote required finding my way through a gray zone, acknowledging the arguments on both sides and doing what I thought was right. Most days, that meant letting somebody down. If I had their cell phone number, I tried to give them a call and walk them through my dilemma. At the very least they appreciated the call, and sometimes they'd admit that they would have made the same decision, too.

25

Stop Calling Mitch McConnell.
Start Calling Your State Representative.

The months of my first term raced by, and before I knew it the session had already passed the halfway point. With our proposals for tolls and free community college paused in legislative limbo, I worried about whether I would actually manage to accomplish any of the ambitious goals I had publicized when running for office. While I had contributed to small wins like banning plastic bags or securing $20 million for the repair of a local bridge, my friends and family didn't seem to notice. Who could blame them? President Trump was talking about buying Greenland and Special Counsel Robert Mueller was investigating Russian interference in the 2016 election.

Scrolling through Instagram reassured me that my friends were still fired up about politics. But I grimaced when I saw them sharing the phone number for Mitch McConnell's office, or the White House switchboard. Anyone who has worked on Capitol Hill knows what happens when a non-constituent calls a member of Congress. Some unpaid intern, trying not to make audible chewing noises as they eat their lunch, will listen to your rant for a polite five to ten minutes, then pretend to have some reason to end the conversation. If you live in another state, no record of the call is made, and Mitch McConnell will go about his day without ever knowing you dropped him a line. Flooding a congressional office with phone calls doesn't really change anything except for an intern's lunch plans.

Now that I worked in Hartford, I had learned what a difference those same calls could make if they were directed at the state level. I wondered why, rather than yelling at a well-trained, courteous nineteen-year-old, more people didn't call their local lawmaker's cell phone. Every so often, those calls changed everything.

Take the issue of student loan debt. Connecticut has the highest student debt per capita in the country, averaging over $30,000 a head. Many people are struggling to pay off bills that are several times higher. When I arrived in Hartford, I requested that non-partisan analysts write a report on how other states addressed the student loan crisis. One major benefit of working in state politics is that you can look at what's worked (and what hasn't) elsewhere. As it turned out, thirty-five states had enacted some sort of student loan tax credit to help recent graduates climb their way out of debt. Although Connecticut had tried to create a few narrow tax credits (such as the Nursing Education Loan Forgiveness Program), most of them had never been implemented.

James Maroney, Alex Kasser, and I wanted to try something new. We believed that addressing the student loan crisis wasn't just the right thing to do for young people—it was a necessary component of reviving our economy. As the leadership of GE had made clear, businesses were having trouble recruiting young people to work in Connecticut, and we hoped that some form of student loan relief might inspire more recent graduates to start their careers here.

As three senators from moderate districts, we knew that Connecticut couldn't afford to abolish trillions of dollars of student debt with the snap of a finger. As awesome as it would be to free millions of people from crushing bills, our state was already low on cash. Searching for a solution, we turned to the private sector. What if more businesses in Connecticut offered student loan relief as part of their employee benefit package? Just as any job applicant considers health care and other benefits when weighing their offers, maybe young people would be drawn to Connecticut if the jobs here offered some level of loan repayment.

Most businesses weren't going to provide this benefit out of the goodness of their hearts. To entice them, Senator Kasser wrote SB 72, a corporate tax credit for any business that helped to pay off their employees' student loans. It was capped at $5,250 per year, per Senator Maroney's suggestion. This synced with a federal tax credit that had been proposed by Connecticut's federal delegation. Once we secured the support of Senator John Fonfara, chair of the Finance Committee, Senator Kasser spearheaded the debate on the floor. Republicans loved the bill because it cut taxes for businesses. Democrats loved it because it helped young people afford their college degrees. SB 72 sailed through the Senate, but the battle was only half over.

The House, with 151 members, is a more chaotic chamber than the Senate. While you can hear a pin drop in the Senate, the House is always filled with the cacophony of floor speeches, side conversations, and gavel pounding. Walk into the chamber and you'll find a lawmaker shouting into the microphone and defending a bill while their colleagues chat with one another at full volume, unfazed by the official business taking place. Whereas the Senate is defined by the Republican caucus and the Democratic caucus, the House is subdivided into smaller caucuses: moderate Democrats, progressives, women, Black, and Puerto Rican lawmakers, to name a few. Since they don't discuss every bill beforehand like the Senate does, there are plenty of antics and surprises on the floor. One day, I was standing near the majority leader's desk when a high-ranking Republican left his huddle of conservatives and walked over to the high-ranking Democrat. He started waving his hands wildly.

"I need to show those guys that I'm pissed at you, so I'm waving my hands. It would be good if you could look angry at me as well," he said. The majority leader didn't miss a beat, making small talk with the Republican as he threw up his hands in faux anger. On the other side of the room, the conservative huddle looked satisfied that their emissary had given the Democrats hell. Showmanship is a big part of this messy process.

Even though SB 72 had passed the Senate easily, Kasser, Maroney, and I were having trouble getting our bill called for a vote in the House. To build momentum, we enlisted the help of the realtors. Most realtors strongly support student debt relief, since student loans delay the purchase of a first home in Connecticut by an average of seven years. In short, reducing debt meant selling more houses. Every community has a handful of realtors, and their lobbyist has an almost frightening ability to mobilize the group when necessary. So we asked him to mobilize in support of SB 72.

Once the realtors were activated, state representatives started to receive calls, texts, and emails from back home about SB 72. Standing in the House chamber, Kasser, Maroney, and I witnessed an avalanche of momentum. Calls weren't screened by an intern but went directly to the legislators themselves. Emails landed right in their inboxes. Democratic and Republican members of the House started to add their names as cosponsors, and soon the bill was called for a vote. When one Republican rose to make the bill a "talker," Tom O'Dea, married to a realtor, rushed over to let him know that this bill was a good one. It passed 138-8.

The next morning, Alex and I stopped by the governor's office and asked him to sign SB 72 into law. Still devoid of pretension, the governor glanced at his senior advisor.

"Do we like that bill?"

"The realtors love it," the advisor responded. On my twenty-third birthday, SB 72 became law.

The capitol was frequently a snarl of negotiations and competing priorities, but a direct phone call from a constituent could go a long way toward moving a vote in the right direction. As the session got busier, the calls that I received helped draw my attention to bills that otherwise might have flown under the radar. And other times, simply hearing someone's voice brought back the human side of politics.

When I was in elementary school, one of my best friends lived two houses down the street. Our moms sometimes arranged for us to carpool after school, and we even went on a ski weekend together. My friend later went to a private high school, and sadly we lost touch. But after I won, her mom developed an odd habit of commenting nasty things on my Facebook page. I'd always known she was a Republican, but I was pretty shocked to see her take part in mean-spirited name-calling. Keep in mind, I hadn't seen this woman since I was a kid in the back of her minivan. After one particularly harsh and personal comment, I remembered that I still had her phone number. Driving home from Hartford that night, I decided to give her a call. "Hi there, I hope you're doing well!" my message started. "I just wanted to make sure you still had my cell phone number, so if you have any feedback on my work in Hartford, you can always reach out. We may disagree, but I'm trying my best." Before I hung up, I added, "Please tell your daughter I say hi!" She never returned my call, but she took a hiatus from my Facebook page for a few months.

As I came to better understand my job as a state senator, I realized how accessible state and local policymakers really are. Citizens who care about protecting access to reproductive health care, addressing climate change, or making college more affordable might be surprised to find that reaching out to their state representatives is a much better use of their time than leaving voicemails for Congress or posting harsh comments on social media. Those conversations with constituents make all the difference in getting a bill across the finish line.

26

College Nights at the Capitol

As our June 5th deadline grew closer, the capitol shifted into overdrive. Only a few days from Sine Die, the fate of my legislative priorities still hung in suspense. *Sine die* (pronounced "sin-ay dee-ay") is a Latin term that means "without day," and it signifies the adjournment of the legislature after a whirlwind six months. As we approached that finish, the dam started to break and bills passed like dominoes. Legislators who had refused to compromise for months suddenly feared that their bills would die an unceremonious death unless they cut a deal.

For those of us who don't serve as caucus leaders, working out those deals involved a tremendous amount of sitting around. Why the long wait? Sometimes the Speaker of the House and the Senate president were still negotiating which bills will be added to a consent calendar. Sometimes the Republicans were caucusing, or the Legislative Commissioners' Office hadn't finished drafting an amendment. Before an amendment reaches the floor, two secretaries literally sit down and read it out loud to compare it with existing statute.

Those of us who wanted our bills to pass but weren't in the room to fight for them distracted ourselves in the Freshman Dorm. Senator Anwar, always a calm voice of reason, taught us to meditate, and

Senator Lesser led a freshman expedition up a secret staircase inside the capitol dome. We tiptoed through a creepy attic and started to climb a winding staircase when the capitol police caught up to us. We must have tripped an alarm, and the officer who chased us looked annoyed and out of breath by the time he found our group. He seemed a little surprised by who he found trespassing.

"Uh, I found about a third of the Senate up here," he sighed into his radio. "Bringing them down now."

Passing time at the capitol wasn't always a partisan endeavor. One night, the members of the Judiciary Committee were putting in long hours in a hearing about whether or not ghost guns should be banned in Connecticut. Ghost guns are firearms that are ordered online and then arrive through the mail in multiple pieces. They don't include a serial number, making it nearly impossible to trace them. Worst of all, their owners aren't subject to a background check.

My conservative colleagues on the committee hated the bill, because in their eyes a gun wasn't a gun until it could shoot bullets. We wanted to track and trace the components of a gun, and that struck them as absurd. But to demonstrate just how dangerous these components could be, Jeremy Stein, an advocate against gun violence, brought an 80 percent lower receiver into the hearing room. It scared the hell out of legislators, because it looked a lot like a gun. That was Jeremy's point—this soon-to-be-gun should be regulated.

"Did you ask anyone for permission to bring that into the building?" the top Republican on the committee asked. Stein said that he had spoken with capitol police, but nothing prevented a member of the public from bringing this scary-looking machinery into the building since it wasn't considered a firearm.

Representative Craig Fishbein, perhaps the legislature's most conservative member, chimed in. He wanted to know why Jeremy felt he had the right to bring the lower receiver into the capitol building. "I guess you're trying to make us believe it's just a chunk of metal?" he asked.

"No," Jeremy responded, a bit exasperated. "That's not what I'm asking you to believe." He wanted us to believe the opposite, and the Republicans proved our point by asking that the gun be removed from the room.

Then, the debate grew even more absurd. One Republican senator worried that "it's hard to determine when a chunk of metal is or is not a gun." It wasn't too hard—the legislation before us clearly established a threshold for when the components of a gun ought to be considered a firearm. But my colleagues knew that. This ridiculous round of questioning was a performance for the Second Amendment fan club in the back row of the hearing room. My toes clenched with frustration. Preventing gun violence had been a mainstay of my campaign, and sitting beside the gun enthusiasts in the audience were the friends and family members of those who had died from a gunshot wound.

A friend on the committee texted me to let me know that pizza had been delivered to a nearby conference room. When I walked in, I was more than a little surprised to find the "chunk of metal" caucus sitting side by side and sharing jokes with the fiercest advocates for gun control. I looked with skepticism at Senator Gary Winfield, the chair of the committee and someone whose conscience I trusted. These guys were trying to kill our bill, and now we were going to share a pizza? Gary gave me a knowing look and shrugged. Impossible as it may sometimes seem, legislating requires setting aside policy disagreements and learning to shoot the breeze together. Even when you're fighting like hell in the other room.

Quite frankly, the stamina of my colleagues amazed me. I figured I was through with all-nighters when I graduated from college. As a student, I had my routine down: I needed a Citrus Lime 5-hour Energy, an eerily silent floor of the library, and a long nap the next day. But the legislature would pull an all-nighter, skip the 5-hour Energy, and then get right back to work. If the Senate was still debating at 4 a.m., the entire building hummed with activity just as it had twelve hours earlier. In fact, the capitol police kept the building fully open to the public. I'm embarrassed to say that I struggled to keep up. During one late night, Senator Len Fasano waved me over to his desk. Len was the top Republican in the Senate, and he carried with him a decency that wasn't exactly omnipresent in this business. His hand-on-the-shoulder and slap-on-the-back approach to creating public policy broke the tension in the most fraught and partisan moments. I found it easy to forget that his job was to figure out how to unseat Democratic state senators like me. Freshman Democrats don't spend a lot of time talking to top Republicans, so I was more than a little nervous when he waved me over to his desk.

"I'm going to delete this photo, but I want you to be more careful," he said.

I had no idea what he was talking about, but I figured an embarrassing Snapchat from college was about to derail my career.

"You've got to watch out for stuff like this," he continued as he handed me his phone.

It turns out, I'd fallen asleep in my chair. Len teased that as the youngest member of the Senate, I didn't have any excuses for dozing off.

"If you need to take a nap, use my office!" he said.

Naps were one option, although I had to be careful. Every few hours, Republicans would introduce an amendment that controverted whatever bill we were debating in some way. When the amendment was called for a vote, senators from both parties would emerge from their slumber and make their way into the chamber. Only the most experienced senators, like longtime Waterbury state senator Joan Hartley, would comb through the details of each amendment. Mostly, these votes fell along party lines.

When taking a nap wouldn't do, I would take a few of Senator Needleman's caffeinated fizzy tablets. Those pills worked so well that I had trouble falling asleep even after I made it back home to Westport. And as a fail-safe option, I could always spend the night on the couch in my office. This wasn't a pleasant experience, since some of the lights in the building never seemed to turn off. But the capitol is equipped with a small locker room where legislators can shower. I'd wake up extra early so that I was dressed and ready before the building started filling up with lobbyists and legislators.

On May 15th, we debated the TRUST Act for eight hours, eventually passing a bill that limited Connecticut's participation in federal deportations. I had been drawn to state government as an opportunity to fight back against President Trump's cruelest policies, and this bill provided an historic opportunity to do just that.

The next day, we passed the Paid Family and Medical Leave Act, a new policy to ensure that no one was forced to choose between their family and their career. At thousands of doors and hundreds of meet and greets, I had shared the story of my single, working mom. Now I had the chance to vote on a policy that would make life just a little easier for parents like her.

A few hours later, we passed the Time's Up Act, extending the statute of limitations for sexual assault and fostering safe workplaces for all. The Me Too movement had inspired countless women in Connecticut and across the country to share their stories of workplace harassment, and now we had an opportunity to echo those voices on the Senate floor and demand change.

The following day, we voted to raise the hourly minimum wage to $15. That filibuster lasted six hours in the Senate and fourteen in the House. As we watched Senator Kushner answer a litany of questions, we were giddy with excitement in the Freshman Dorm. Unlike so many legislative reforms, this bill didn't create a study about whether or not to increase funding for a program that might eventually help a constituent. It would have a direct impact, guaranteeing Connecticut workers a raise. Most of these workers were women, and many were currently supporting a family on just $10.10 an hour. When the bill finally passed, we took our adrenaline over to Red Rock, a nearby bar frequented by Capitol-types. As we toasted

to Senator Kushner, someone held up a hot-off-the-press cover of the
next morning's paper. We'd raised the minimum wage just in time to
meet the *Hartford Courant*'s printing deadline. Mae pulled me aside
and reminded me that each of these reforms had been stalled when
the Senate was tied.

Finally, on the day before Sine Die, the state budget landed on our
desks. With only a few hours to review the comprehensive document
before casting my vote, I raced through the line items to see if my
top priority was included. After scanning pages of appropriations,
I finally saw that free community college was funded. My heart
raced with the feeling that I had actually gotten something done. I
thought about the food pantries that Gregg and I had seen on every
community college campus and hoped that students would have
an easier time affording their next meal now that they didn't have
to worry about tuition. After casting my vote at around 10 p.m., I
thought about calling my friends or family to share the good news.
But it was late, and it would have taken too long to explain just how
many obstacles this policy had encountered. Instead, I hugged my
new friends in the caucus room.

When June 5th finally arrived, hundreds of bills had yet to receive
a vote with twenty-four hours to go. Of course, bills need to pass
both the House and the Senate in order to reach the governor's desk
and become law. If they've passed through only one chamber, they
wither and die at the stroke of midnight. By this point, dozens of
bills that passed in the House had yet to be called in the Senate,
and dozens of bills that passed the Senate had yet to be called in the
House. Now the chambers didn't have enough time to debate and
vote on each bill as a stand-alone item. A grand bargain needed to
be reached, whereby some of the House bills awaiting a vote would
be added to a Senate consent calendar, and vice versa. If a bill failed
to make it onto that consent calendar, it was toast.

It takes only a single senator's objection to keep a bill off of
the coveted consent calendar, which meant that Republicans and

Democrats now effectively had equal power. To prevent Republicans from objecting to the bills we liked, we needed to add a fair number of the bills they liked. It was a hostage situation.

As this high-stakes negotiation pressed on, I was surprised that HB 5001 was taking center stage.

"That's a placeholder bill," I replied when Courtney texted to ask if I was okay adding it to the consent calendar. Placeholder bills don't have any substance, so I didn't understand why anyone would be fighting for that bill in the final hours of the session. HB 5001, titled *An Act Requiring the Study of the Workforce Training Needs in the State*, created a task force that probably already existed. But HB 5001 arrived in the Senate with an amendment that was completely unrelated to the workforce training needs of Connecticut, or higher education at all for that matter. My more seasoned colleagues called this a "rat."

Rats are unattractive public policies, snuck into bills with the hope that no one would notice. This particular rat allowed restaurants to get away with paying their employees the tipped minimum wage ($6.38) when they should have been paying the full minimum wage (soon to be $15). In Connecticut, restaurants can pay waitstaff the lower wage whenever they have an opportunity to earn tips. But hours spent cleaning the bathroom or stocking supplies needed to be compensated at the regular minimum wage, since this sort of work didn't bring in tips. Restaurant managers are required to maintain complete and accurate records about which hours the employees spent doing which sort of work.

Top Republicans in the House wanted to appease the restaurants in their district, and the Democrats had quietly gone along with a deal that exposed countless restaurant workers to the risk of being underpaid. I wasn't in the room (or, more likely, the hallway) when the handshake happened, but I imagine the House Democrats must have gotten a lot of their bills passed in exchange for this bad policy. Even my most progressive friends looked the other way when supporting the bill. This subject was well outside of my usual policy portfolio, but it smelled fishy and I wasn't eager to support it. That said, tanking this bill would have disrupted the grand bargain.

Around 11:30 p.m., Senator Bob Duff, the Senate majority leader, morphed into an auctioneer. Bob sits directly to my left, and I had learned a ton from watching him run the floor on a daily basis. As the second-highest-ranking Democrat in the Senate, he and his staff ensure smooth operations every day, wielding the phone on his desk to check in with other leaders in the chamber and hash out which bill is up next and who will speak on it. Bob is mild-mannered and generous with his time, often passing along a trick of the trade or a bit of insider knowledge. We regularly carpooled up to the capitol together, chatting the whole way about the business that lay ahead. But on Sine Die, he became the final arbitrator of what became law and what didn't. With all eyes on him and the clock ticking, he announced the final fifty or so bills to make it across the finish line. The railing of the Senate was lined with House members who were fighting tooth and nail to get their priorities on Bob's list.

The clock struck midnight, and the session was over. And then, strangely enough, both parties started to party apolitically. After months of fighting like hell, Democrats and Republicans dropped their guard and shared toasts. Governor Lamont delivered an after-hours speech, congratulating the legislature on a productive session and inviting lawmakers to his office for a drink. Alex Romanowicz, who had been through Sine Die many times before, helped me recover from the whiplash.

"You're going to need to work with these people next year, so there's no sense holding a grudge," he said. Suddenly, Republicans who had opposed the Paid Family and Medical Leave Act now offered to pour us a beer. Reporters whom I had learned to keep at arm's length were now competing with lawmakers over who could land a Hula-Hoop, tossed from the railing of the fourth floor, around the first-floor statue of Nathan Hale. Aides brought out Jell-O shots and taught the older senators how to move their finger around the cup and dislodge the goo. "It has the texture of an oyster," one of my colleagues noted. Doors inside the capitol that were previously closed to Democrats, like the Republican conference room, swung open. Inside the Speaker's suite, Alex beat me handily in beer pong. All of a sudden, life in the legislature felt a little like college.

But I'd become so invested in this job that I had trouble relaxing alongside House Republicans who might be planning to run against me in the next election, or Senate colleagues who had opposed including free prison phone calls in the budget. Plus, all of this levity felt like a disservice to the constituents who had sent me here. Was it really appropriate to celebrate despite the fact that we hadn't made a real dent in health care costs, hadn't figured out how to fund transportation, and failed to address racial segregation between cities and suburbs?

My wiser colleagues reminded me that we'd be back in six months or so, and those issues would be on the table once again. In the meantime, I needed to recognize that Republican legislators were fighting for their communities and their beliefs just like I was fighting for mine. We might disagree on policy, but we all earned the same small salary and worked the same long hours. Passing those laws in the next session required strong relationships. It may seem strange, but kicking back together after the clock struck midnight was just one more part of the process.

I still have my hesitations. The work of the legislature is a kind of business, but it's not "just" business, really. We have long, heated debates not for the sport of it but, hopefully, recognizing that the laws we pass impact the details of our constituents' everyday lives. We don't disagree only on minute policy details, but sometimes on fundamental questions about what sort of future we want for our state and who should get to share in it. It's my job to work with Republicans and others I disagree with, because it's my job to compromise and get laws across the finish line. But I'm not sure whether the job should involve sharing toasts together when we have drastically different things to celebrate.

EPILOGUE

27

You Should Run for Office

The temperature was climbing inside my Subaru Forester. Ever since I'd introduced a bill to crack down on unnecessary idling, I was a stickler about keeping my car off and avoiding unnecessary carbon emissions. But I was starting to sweat in the familiar parking lot outside the Wilton Library. Inside, a modest crowd of hard-core Democrats and hard-core Republicans were waiting for my first town hall meeting after the session to start. Before I walked in, I needed to review my notes. I'd cast more than 600 votes over the last six months, and I knew I'd be challenged to defend many of them.

When I reached the podium, I looked at my constituents and fessed up that they probably didn't agree with every decision I had made. On the screen behind me, I shared a photograph that I had taken of my desk shortly before voting on the $43.4 billion budget, and pointed out the green "Yea" button and the red "Nay" button. I argued that working in the capitol involved countless hard choices and two inflexible options.

I spoke about gun violence prevention, pension obligations, transportation infrastructure, and renewable energy. I tried to be transparent about where I'd made progress and where I would push harder next year. I thanked Governor Lamont for vetoing HB 5001, the "rat." As strange as it seemed, rejoicing in the death of a bill I had helped to pass summed up how my first year of legislating was filled with paradoxes and crappy choices. If the Senate hadn't approved HB 5001 that night, the House might not have passed SB 750, which increased access to mental health services on college campuses, or SB 832, which cracked down on elder abuse and neglect. On Sine Die, political considerations had superseded policy concerns as we hurtled toward the midnight finish line.

When it came time for questions, the Democrats asked what we had done to make voting more accessible and Republicans asked whether or not I raised any taxes. One gentleman asked if I knew Connecticut's state motto, and I silently thanked Ms. Ellaneous as I recited the Latin (*Qui Transtulit Sustinet*) and the English (He Who Transplanted Still Sustains).

The question that caught me off guard had nothing to do with the votes I had studied in my car beforehand. It was basic and nonpartisan. A student in the back row raised her hand and asked: "Does the system work?"

My first reaction was an unequivocal yes. I decided to run for office because I'd lost faith in politics, and only a few months later I claimed a seat at the table. After knocking on thousands of doors, I had won the opportunity to make community college free, enact stronger gun regulations, and ban plastic bags. My first short bill about Wi-Fi on Metro-North had ensured that the Department of Transportation included connectivity improvements in their plans to upgrade commuter rail lines. Every day, I had an opportunity to walk the halls of power and plan for the future of our state.

But those halls were lined by white, male policy makers who looked a lot like me. I was tired of being the youngest person in every room, and I was fed up with lobbyists who spouted beliefs that they were paid to hold. I hated telling constituents that a critically important bill hadn't passed because arbitrary and self-imposed deadlines had caused us to "run out of time." I was frustrated that meetings were always scheduled on top of each other, making it impossible to dig into the substantive work of each committee. I was burned out from all of the late nights and painfully aware that single moms like mine would struggle to hold a job with such irregular hours. I was broke and wondering how long I could afford to be a state senator.

Politicians often trot out a tired quote that Otto von Bismarck didn't actually say: "If you like laws and sausages, you should never watch either one being made." That may be unfair to the fine men and women who make sausages. In fact, Stanley A. Feder, president of Simply Sausage, told the *New York Times* in 2010 that he is "so insulted" by the comparison. After all, Feder's team carefully vets ingredients and adheres to strict quality control. Those safeguards are lacking in the legislative process.

Despite all of these shortcomings, I think it's fair to say that the system works, because President Obama was right: voters who are disappointed in their elected officials can indeed pick up a clipboard and run for office themselves. Those of us who do so have the responsibility of making it just a little easier for the next candidate to take that leap of faith. Political insiders thought it was absurd for me to seek a seat in the state Senate, but my community decided to give me a chance. Thankfully, the voters call the shots in a democracy. Although politics may seem inaccessible, or fatally flawed, or simply useless, I've seen firsthand how the system we all like to decry still allows ordinary people to make change.

Anyone who doubted the importance of government—particularly state government—has probably changed their tune over the last two years. In March 2020, Westport became the very first COVID-19 hot spot in Connecticut. Completely oblivious to the work that lay ahead, I complained that the legislature had canceled meetings for the next few days. Important reforms, including a bill I was working to pass that would provide students with more opportunities to report sexual misconduct on campus, had been put on hold. Jack was back in Connecticut, preparing for my reelection campaign, which was only eight months away. With critical votes delayed, he was worried that I wouldn't have a robust record of legislative accomplishment to effectively make the case that I deserved another term. But as the virus escalated and the death toll started to rise, we forgot all about the campaign and the pending legislation.

There is no playbook to follow when it comes to serving your community during a pandemic. Without any norms to guide us, we found new ways to communicate with constituents and lend a hand. Instead of hosting in-person town halls, I went live on Facebook to answer questions about the capacity at local hospitals and loans that were available to small-business owners. We used Instagram to educate young people about how their decision to stay home would protect their parents and grandparents. In record numbers, constituents reached out for help. They needed tests, masks, Plexiglas, rental assistance, unemployment benefits, and more. Many people had never contacted a government official before. Some told me that they didn't realize they had a state senator, and others divulged that they disagreed with most of my political positions. Alex and I fought for each one of them, contacting the appropriate state agency and pleading on their behalf. Our telephone town halls drew thousands of listeners, and we'd work through hundreds of voicemails the next morning from those whose questions I didn't have a chance to answer. On good days, we found housing for homeless constituents, and on bad days we spoke to tearful constituents who desperately wanted to visit their loved one in a nursing home.

Jack transitioned our campaign team into a COVID response unit, training dozens of high school and college students to check in on local seniors instead of asking for their votes. The young people who worked for us, sad not to be in school but full of energy, spent their afternoons calling elderly neighbors to see how they were faring. After a few weeks, they had reached over 10,000 constituents and brightened the days of those who were struggling with isolation. The students told me that the calls made them happy, too. If a constituent lacked access to groceries or medication, we connected them with a social worker. When one gentleman in Bethel told us he needed a cane to stay balanced while moving around the house, I picked one out and drove it to his front door.

My job couldn't have been more different in the absence of press conferences or late-night filibusters, but this work was more satisfying than passing any law in Hartford had been. When seemingly all else failed, the government was stepping up to assist people who were struggling. My conservative colleagues often quote President Reagan's famous quip: "The nine most terrifying words in the English language are: I'm from the government, and I'm here to help." Sure, the public sector can be bureaucratic and inefficient. But some elected officials just lack the imagination to consider all the ways in which the government can touch people's lives. Before bed each night, I wrote personal notes to families who had lost a loved one due to COVID-19 and kids who had to cancel their birthday parties due to social distancing requirements. Unclear what exactly a state senator should be doing during an unprecedented time, our team did anything and everything that we could think of.

As November got closer, a local accountant from Wilton announced that she was running against me. Her pitch was pretty simple: the Twenty-Sixth District had made a mistake by electing a kid, and it was time to put the adults back in charge. She won the endorsement of the police unions and claimed that the state budget numbers "don't add up." I started to see her signs appear in front yards across the district, and I worried once again that perhaps my victory had been a fluke. Maybe the voters had made a mistake in 2018, and I wasn't actually good at my job. Like many young people in politics, I felt like an impostor, frequently doubting whether or not I was able to do what was now expected of me. In Hartford, that feeling inspired me to work harder, cosponsoring twenty-three new laws and bringing back millions of dollars for my towns. Now

I realized that it wasn't the bills I had passed or the funding I procured that made me a good senator. It was the hours spent helping people, and the creative ways that our team reached out to apolitical constituents who needed resources. Maybe I was a good state senator not in spite of my age but because of it.

By the time the debates rolled around, I was surprised to realize that I wasn't nervous to go head-to-head with my opponent. I knew the policy issues by now, and I didn't need to be an accountant to know that the state budget did, in fact, add up. But more importantly, the notion that I was too young to serve the community seemed absurd, as our team was helping hundreds of people every day. Once again, I figured out that I was up to the job by . . . doing the job.

On November 3rd, Jack, Alex, and I breathed a sigh of relief into our masks when the Twenty-Sixth District gave me the opportunity to serve for another two years. Satisfied with the work I was doing, almost 60 percent of voters had given me the nod for a second term. We had won six out of seven towns, surpassing our most ambitious expectations. Here in Connecticut and across the country, youth turnout had delivered a victory for Democrats. And after the election was over, many of the same interns who had made check-in calls during the campaign picked up their phones once again, this time to help seniors sign up for a vaccine appointment.

An acknowledgment is growing, especially in Democratic circles, that young people make good candidates. We outwork our opponents, bring new voters into the fold, and speak to issues that the establishment politicians often ignore. It should come as no surprise, then, that young people make good public servants after Election Day is over. We find new ways to connect with our constituents and turn our lives over to the job. Across the country, in red states and blue states, young elected officials inspire me to do more and do better. The world watched as Lina Hidalgo, a county judge in Texas, took bold steps to protect her community from COVID-19 when other elected officials in Texas weren't taking the science seriously.

Young state senators like Mallory McMorrow in Michigan, Raumesh Akbari in Tennessee, Sarah McBride in Delaware, and Megan Hunt in Nebraska fight for the next generation on Twitter and on their respective Senate floors.

Probably every worker is eager to please their boss. But the pressure is greater when dealing with your first boss, since they've taken an especially big chance on you. With 100,000 first bosses, I worried constantly about delivering for a community that had done something crazy by sending a twenty-two-year-old into the state Senate. Thankfully, I soon learned that public policy isn't created by PhDs who know everything about every issue. Instead, laws are written by overworked and underpaid public servants who simply try to keep up with the chaotic legislative process and give voice to the values of their neighbors. Theoretically, these legislators represent the diversity of the people they represent. But in reality, young people are absent from the lawmaking process. As a result, the present takes precedence over the future.

Nowadays, when my phone rings with a call from an unfamiliar area code, I know the caller is likely a student who is on the verge of running for office. They've got their eye on a school board seat in Arizona, a state senate seat in Florida, a city council seat in Alabama. I try my best to answer their practical questions about how to build a campaign, but I spend most of the call simply encouraging them to follow their instincts. Many of their neighbors will claim they aren't up for the job, but I can guarantee that as a young candidate, they'll bring a new set of skills and insights to make our government better. The system works, I assure them. But only if they decide to run.

28

When Optimism Arrives in the Voting Booth

Elections in 2018 and 2020 proved that young people are a force to be reckoned with in American politics. The United States Elections Project found that 36 percent of citizens aged eighteen to twenty-nine reported voting in the 2018 midterms. For a group that often opts to stay home during nonpresidential elections, this amounted to an astounding increase. Compared with the 2014 midterm elections, turnout increased 16 percentage points. And when they reached the polls, these newly energized voters overwhelmingly supported Democrats. In Georgia, 63 percent of eighteen- to twenty-nine-year-olds supported gubernatorial candidate Stacey Abrams, and in Texas 71 percent in that same age group supported Senate candidate Beto O'Rourke.

They returned to the polls in record numbers in 2020, with 52–55 percent of eligible voters in that age group casting a ballot. That amounted to roughly a 10 percent increase since the last presidential election. Young voters in Michigan, Georgia, Arizona, and Pennsylvania favored Joe Biden and helped secure the necessary Electoral College votes to defeat Donald Trump. When it came to young people showing up, the 2018 midterms weren't an anomaly but instead marked the beginning of a new normal.

But most pundits still get it wrong when they talk about young voters. They focus on millennials and overlook a younger group that has just entered the fold. Although it's easy to group millennials and Gen Z together, doing so ignores the fact that these groups walk into the voting booth with dramatically different worldviews. While generational cutoffs are far from scientific, millennials are typically defined as those born before 1996. They owned a Walkman and fluently texted with the awkward keys of a flip phone. And in their relatively short lifetime, they've experienced two epic recessions and witnessed as many decades of unnecessary war. Like the country itself, they are deeply in debt, and are, according to one paper from the Brookings Institution, the least-trusting of any generation. In 2012, only 19 percent of millennials agreed that, generally speaking, most people can be trusted. That degree of cynicism stands in stark contrast to the unguarded baby boomers, 40 percent of whom agreed that most people can be trusted. If we thought that skepticism of the government peaked with the burning of bras and draft cards in the 1960s, millennials upped the ante by wondering why anyone bothered to protest anything anyway. In fact, a 2014 study from the University of Georgia found that Congress had a higher approval among boomers during the Vietnam era than it does among millennials today.

By contrast, eighteen- to twenty-four-year-olds are joining the electorate with optimism. In Connecticut's Twenty-Sixth Senate District and across the country, the very youngest voters see themselves as part of a team that can reform or replace the status quo. The Center for Information and Research on Civic Learning and Engagement's (CIRCLE) 2018 poll found that 81 percent of Gen Z members believe young people have the power to institute change. Somehow, the first two years of Trump's presidency only made us more hopeful. While Washington, DC, was paralyzed by partisanship, young people walked out of school to demand stricter gun laws and went on a global strike for climate justice. Trump may have mocked teen activist Greta Thunberg for "anger management issues," but young activists followed her lead and came to see politics as an effective avenue for fixing the world they inherited. In 2016, 7 percent of eighteen- to twenty-four-year-olds disagreed with the statement "I don't think public officials care much about what people like me think." By 2018, the number that disagreed grew to 18 percent. Increased youth turnout in the midterms reflected our generation's hope that we could change not only what public officials cared about but also who got to be a public official.

How is it possible that optimism is the defining characteristic of a generation that grew up during the Forever Wars of the Bush era, rehearsed dozens of school shooter drills, watched the rise of a reality-TV star to the Oval Office, and spent more than a year indoors due to a virus that caused the worst recession since the Great Depression? Perhaps the confidence of Gen Z stems from the realization that the status quo is untenable, so sweeping change is inevitable. Any discussion of generational politics is unavoidably laced with generalizations, but the millennials I know seem to think they can squeak by in the crappy system as it currently exists. Many have followed the conventional framework set out by prior generations—go to college, maybe grad school, try to work for a good company, and hope things work out. They may understand that their generation will likely be one of the first that falls behind their parents, but many think that they can individually be the exception to that rule. Just look at the paradox unearthed by two surveys: in 2012, the Pew Research Center found that 83 percent of millennials agreed that "there is too much power concentrated in the hands of a few big companies." But at the same time, the consulting company Universum polled employed millennials on where they'd most like to work. Google, Facebook, Amazon, Apple, and Disney all scored near the top. While millennials may agree that these companies have too much power, they'd like to work for them nonetheless. In other words, millennials hope to enjoy the trappings of conventional success without changing the underlying issues that make such success impossible for most of their peers.

Even from my seat on the blurry line between the two generations, I can see an unmistakable trend of Gen Z leaders who recognize that they have no prayer of squeaking by in the current system. Oil reserves will be gone in about fifty years, meaning we'll need to find a new way to power our world. By 2050, 150 million people will be displaced by rising sea levels, and many of the world's coastal cities will be underwater. If college tuition continues rising at the current rate, the cost of a year at the average private college will surpass $120,000 by 2035. We know that the fever has to break, so we're ready to be a part of the solution.

The Democratic establishment has spent decades hand-wringing about whether the path to victory runs through moderate suburban voters who need to be persuaded or through progressive activists who need to be mobilized. I don't claim to know the answer, but I'd suggest that any path to victory must be paved by young voters. The 2018 midterms were a wake-up call to Democrats that young people are a crucial part of their coalition. Luckily for the Left, we're still growing—literally, in some cases. But in a party led by septuagenarians and their more senior colleagues, Democrats will need to figure out how to harness this opportunity and maximize the potential of this emerging electorate.

First, I'd recommend taking young people and their policy priorities seriously. For years, candidates have spent time talking about young voters instead of talking to them. They posed for photo ops in classrooms but didn't hire any young advisors who might spearhead a student loan reform proposal. As Gen Z becomes increasingly political, candidates will need to do a better job of building campaigns that are managed by young people, not just marketed to them. Remember the most cringeworthy ad of the 2020 presidential cycle? In a short clip aimed at young people, a U.S. senator threw a ping-pong ball into a red Solo cup, urging supporters to donate a dollar to her presidential primary campaign if she sank her shot. Though the shot went in, the appeal was widely panned, falling victim to the dreaded coolness paradox.

The coolness paradox rears its head when a candidate tries to win over young people by showing that, despite a generational divide, they are young and hip at heart. Of course, the problem is that the more they try, the more uncool they seem, and we're left with inauthentic pandering. This approach brought us Biden/Harris lawn signs in the virtual world of Animal Crossing.

Young voters aren't looking for the coolest candidate—if they were, they certainly wouldn't have chosen me. Joe Biden probably doesn't know what Animal Crossing is, and that's okay. Young people are looking for politicians who take them seriously. When I visited classrooms in Connecticut, I listened and learned from students who had never been asked how the state government could better serve them. At Weston Middle School, students stood up to a bipartisan panel of candidates and urged us to combat climate change. The Republican candidate sitting next to me pedantically asked the students if they wanted a big, ugly wind turbine in their backyard, then laughed as he handed out his campaign stickers. I spotted one smart seventh grader rolling her eyes in the back row.

Per tradition, Ridgefield High School's senior class invited Boucher and me to participate in a mock debate a few weeks before Election Day. She went on stage carrying an enormous tiger, Ridgefield's mascot. I didn't have any props, but I answered their first question honestly; I supported the legalization of cannabis. I won the mock election, 211 to 54. Young people didn't need stickers or stuffed animals to get fired up about politics. They just needed to know where we stood on the issues.

Second, Democrats must champion policies that facilitate youth participation in the democratic process. Two opportunities stand out as an effective means of increasing Gen Z turnout: implementing automatic voter registration (AVR) and preregistering sixteen-year-olds. AVR entails ditching an opt-in system of voter registration and replacing it with an opt-out system. In other words, eligible citizens are added to the voter rolls unless they choose otherwise. We don't ask citizens to register for their constitutional rights to speak freely or worship a god of their choosing, so why require them to opt in for the chance to vote? AVR has proven to be safe and secure in states across the country, as data collected from the Department of Motor Vehicles, the Department of Social Services, and other state agencies is seamlessly moved onto the voter rolls.

Preregistration allows citizens who are not yet old enough to vote to register in advance of their eighteenth birthday. Sixteen-year-olds who visit the DMV to obtain a driver's license may not interact with state bureaucrats again until their licenses expire in five years or so. Allowing them to preregister during this routine interaction with the government ensures they are equipped to vote once they turn eighteen.

Only a handful of states (California, Colorado, Massachusetts, Maryland, Oregon, Rhode Island, and Washington) have both AVR and preregistration. And, unsurprisingly, young people in those states have responded to these policies by voting in large numbers. The Center for American Progress notes that more than 390,000 Oregonians registered to vote through the AVR program. Between 2016 and 2018, 77,800 voters preregistered, and more than 18,800 turned eighteen in time to cast their first vote in the 2018 midterms.

Same-day registration and early voting are also important policies that help engage young voters. Same-day registration allows citizens to register to vote and cast their ballots in one fell swoop. People who move frequently are especially sensitive to the relative ease or difficulty of registering in a new state and, unsurprisingly, census data confirms that young people move more frequently than their parents or grandparents. Between going to college, finding a job, and starting a family, young adults "have the highest rate of migration" when compared with other age groups, meaning they need to reregister to vote more often. Getting young people to the polls will require tearing down the bureaucratic burdens that too often dilute or obstruct our elections.

Early voting allows the electorate to cast a ballot before Election Day. While states like Connecticut adhere to an antiquated and inconvenient tradition of opening up the polls exclusively on the first Tuesday in November, other states provide many days or even weeks of open polls. Along with single working parents, commuters, individuals with disabilities, and anybody who finds flexibility appealing, young people appreciate the opportunity to vote on a date that is convenient for them. In the states that allowed it, early voting played a critical role in helping young voters cast a ballot in 2018 without missing school or work. According to the Center for American Progress, early voting among eighteen- to twenty-nine-year-olds increased by 188 percent in 2018 compared with 2014.

Sadly, Connecticut lags behind the rest of the country when it comes to the accessibility of our elections. Connecticut's secretary of state, the chief election official, has implemented automatic voter registration voluntarily, but she isn't required to do so by law. In other words, the next secretary of state could decide to stop this vital practice. Our state allows young people to register to vote if they turn eighteen before the next election, but we don't preregister sixteen-year-olds or most seventeen-year-olds. Although Connecticut does offer same-day voter registration, we are one of only ten states in the country that still doesn't permit early voting. Tackling these reforms would surely help more young people reach the polls, building a government that is representative of every generation.

Making elections more convenient shouldn't be controversial in the halls of the state capitol, because surely anyone who decides to run for office believes that democracy functions best when more people participate, not fewer. But while the Senate Democratic caucus spent much of 2019 trying to change our antiquated voting laws, we met stiff opposition from our Republican colleagues. When we debated a constitutional amendment that would allow Connecticut to offer early voting, every Republican but one voted against it. Publicly and privately, I asked them to consider the potential obstacles faced by those in our community who couldn't easily make it to a polling place during limited hours. I was crushed when the bill failed to reach a sufficient majority in the Senate, and I seethed in the Freshman Dorm as Republicans argued on the floor that every citizen could conveniently cast a ballot on Election Day.

So I decided to call their bluff. I proposed that we make voting a civic duty in Connecticut, much like jury duty and the census. Around the world, twenty-six successful democracies already employ civic duty voting, and while we jump up and down about 58 percent turnout for a national election, Australian parliamentary elections regularly see more than 90 percent of eligible voters participating. Adopting this model ensures a government that reflects the will of all the people, not just the people who show up. In 2015, President Barack Obama was asked about how best to address the problem of moneyed interests influencing politics during a town hall at the City Club of Cleveland. He pointed to the civic duty voting model. "In Australia . . . there's mandatory voting," he said. "That would counteract money more than anything. If everybody voted, then it would completely change the political map in this country, because the people who tend not to vote are young; they're lower income; they're skewed more heavily towards immigrant groups and minority groups," Obama went on.

When my bill became public, many of my colleagues lost their minds. With a vigor that I hadn't quite expected, they defended the right *not* to vote as though it were enshrined in the Second Amendment. Even the *Wall Street Journal*'s editorial board weighed in, expressing concern that such a requirement would be unfair to "busy single moms, apolitical 19-year-olds, the homeless . . ." and anyone else who couldn't conveniently make it to the polls.

Suddenly, the Republicans were seemingly concerned about voter access. Without a hint of irony, they flipped from claiming that elections were easily accessible to arguing that our elections were too inaccessible to expect universal turnout. Civic duty voting has the potential to end the centuries-old fight about ballot access, posited an Ash Center/Brookings Institution report titled *Lift Every Voice: The Urgency of Universal Civic Duty Voting.* "To say that everyone should vote is the surest guarantee that everyone will be enabled to vote," the authors explain. In other words, any democracy that views voting as a civic duty must also accept the task of making their elections convenient. If Connecticut treated voting as a civic duty, no policy maker could justify the outdated laws on our books.

My civic duty voting proposal didn't go anywhere, but I was pleased to see my Republican colleagues start to admit that our elections are currently inaccessible or inconvenient to some. The fight over who has convenient access to the ballot has implications beyond which candidates win and lose on Election Day. After all, I've learned that every politician keeps a close eye on their next election. When young people don't show up at the ballot box, their concerns don't show up on our agenda in the Senate. If we want politicians to take their younger constituents seriously, we need to pass reforms that empower young people to vote as reliably as our parents and grandparents do. Until then, issues that matter to elder generations will take precedence over college affordability, environmental protections, or gun violence prevention.

29

Representative Democracy Isn't Representative . . . Yet

Getting young people to the ballot is an important first step. But it's also time to get more young people *on* the ballot. Financial challenges can deter would-be candidates who are unable to compete with deep-pocketed election opponents. Many may be precluded from working in public service when their salaries won't cover loans and rent. While I had Connecticut's campaign funding laws on my side, I found myself in a financial bind after the election.

My New Canaan apartment, I learned, was not actually zoned for residential living. The landlord hadn't disclosed this fact, but the local Republicans started to make hay out of it on social media. Since the apartment was not a legal residence, I had to move out. However, I couldn't afford an apartment of my own. Moving back home wasn't an option, since my mom lived in the small corner of Westport that fell outside of the Twenty-Sixth District. So Marge offered for me to stay in a room off of her garage, where she kept a TV and a pull-out couch.

Marge's offer was a godsend, and I moved in a few days after Election Day. Still, if I ever aspired to living somewhere other than my girlfriend's mom's garage, I'd need to find a second job. Most of my colleagues juggled other jobs outside of the legislature or had recently retired from lucrative careers. Of course, I'd just spent months fighting for my first job, and the prospect of finding another one seemed daunting. Seemingly every potential employer had some business before the state government, and I didn't want to get tied up in anything that smelled of controversy.

Luckily, Congressman Jim Himes needed a scheduler. I'd interned for Jim when I was a high school and college student, and I was excited about the prospect of joining his team. Plus, increased coordination between federal and state officials can only benefit constituents. This was the rare job opportunity without any conflict of interest.

As I considered my next steps, one veteran state senator took me out to dinner and advised me not to take the scheduler job. "Plenty of people in that building already don't take you seriously," he said. "With that job, you'll be viewed as someone's right-hand man."

Perhaps, but Jim needed an answer and I needed a paycheck. I accepted the job and took on the task of managing the congressman's Connecticut schedule. When I wasn't in Hartford, I often drove Jim from place to place. Along the ride, we compared the legislative mechanics of Hartford with Washington, DC. Our political ideology was similar but not identical, so we prodded each other to defend votes that the other had taken. We made hard apple cider in his kitchen, trading bottles and feedback once our respective batches had finally fermented. Jim isn't one for sentimentality, but I came to see him as a role model. Of course I admired his work in Congress. But more importantly, I admired that he was a real person. As his staffer, I saw that he made time for hobbies and family. I had given my life over to being a candidate and then a legislator, dropping everything else that had previously interested me. At some point in the course of shaking hands with people whose names I couldn't remember, I'd forgotten the person I was before I became a politician. Jim also isn't drawn to glad-handing, yet he managed to win reelection every year and move bills through Congress without giving every part of his identity to his job. Jim taught me that politicians could be normal people, too.

By the end of my first legislative session in 2019, I had saved enough to move out of Marge's garage and rent a studio apartment in Westport. But the meager salary of a Connecticut state senator hasn't budged since 2001, effectively shrinking over the decades thanks to inflation. Connecticut ranks twentieth nationally when it comes to legislative pay, although it is admittedly difficult to compare legislator salaries across states since each state capital operates according to its own unique set of rules and procedures. Plus, gridlock in DC has forced every statehouse to do more work than ever to fill a legislative vacuum. So while some states accomplish this work over the course of just one month per year, others meet all year long. Legislators in New Mexico have no salary at all, but those in California take home more than $90,000 a year.

How did Connecticut wind up with such low salaries? Once upon a time, our state's framers envisioned a part-time legislature, filled with farmers, doctors, lawyers, and others who would dedicate their spare time to public service. The quaint promise of a citizen-led legislature, populated with working people who bring professional expertise and insights, is wonderful. Unfortunately, it's far from reality.

Today, some of the people who serve in the legislature cannot afford to feed their families, pay a mortgage, and send their kids to college. This group suffers in silence, since the attack ad against those who propose a pay increase will practically write itself. No one wants to appear ungrateful for the opportunity to serve, and nearly every politician knows not to boost their own salary when other families are struggling to make ends meet. Only Senator Needleman, who doesn't accept a paycheck, dares to speak up on behalf of others.

"I hate to be as crass as to say, 'You get what you pay for,'" he told one reporter. "It's just intuitively obvious that we're excluding a large percentage of the population because we don't pay a reasonable wage," he added. Norm is right. Jessica Post, president of the Democratic Legislative Campaign Committee, works across the country to recruit a diverse set of Democrats to run for the legislature. But these structural barriers thwart the push to diversify. "Many people take a pay cut to run for the state legislature," she told *Politico*. "Compensation is an issue. The schedule of [the] legislative session is an issue. Childcare is an issue," she continued.

In Connecticut and across the country, legislatures have a vast imbalance of independently wealthy individuals, often retired and making a pivot to public service. Others rely on outside employment to pay the bills, which gives an advantage to those with flexible professions, like attorneys, while putting 9-to-5 workers at a disadvantage. Plus, searching for outside employment can cause a host of headaches.

Next time you write a cover letter, try including the caveat that you'll be tied up from January to June. Once the session ends, you'll be ready to report back to work . . . except, of course, you'll need to make sure your constituents remember what you look like after having spent the past six months in Hartford. Since you're up for reelection in no time, you'll need to accept at least a few invitations to ribbon cuttings, or classroom visits, or business tours, or parades. Oh, and most of the 100,000 people you represent have no idea that this is just a six-month gig, so they'll still need help applying for rental assistance or grant funding or fishing licenses. Every so often, and without much warning, you'll need to return to Hartford for a special session to vote on the issues that can't wait until the legislature reconvenes the following January. Before you know it, it's campaign season and you'll need to spend all day knocking on doors. But other than that, you'll be a wonderful employee.

Some legislators have more luck with employers who have

something to gain by cozying up to the state government. Too often, there's a willingness to overlook extended absences in order to have an ally at the capitol. Many lawmakers find themselves working for utility companies, or unions, or nonprofits. Although most of my colleagues excuse themselves when debate begins on a bill that impacts their other job, no enforcement mechanism requires them to do so. In short, failing to pay public servants a living wage can breed corruption or the appearance of corruption. If legislative pay weren't so low, Connecticut lawmakers might consider enacting ethics regulations that limit outside compensation.

In January 2021, the Compensation Commission for Elected State Officers and General Assembly Members met to rethink Connecticut's legislative salaries. To be clear, the commission does not have the authority to actually enact changes, but they meet once every two years to provide a recommendation to the legislature. The group is chaired by Richard Balducci, a lobbyist who previously served as the Speaker of the House. At the meeting, Mary Ann Handley, a former state senator who sits on the commission, noted that "unless we provide a reasonable income for somebody who's going to be a legislator, we're really cutting out a lot of people who can't afford to take this kind of job." To their credit, the group recommended a pay raise . . . of about $300. The next day, the top Republican in the Senate blasted the proposal, calling it "tone deaf." The legislature declined to take up the issue.

One day at a ribbon cutting, a man approached me to complain about the apartment complexes popping up around town. "These buildings, like that one on the Post Road, just destroy the character of our town. And God knows who is moving in there—" I cut him off. "I am! Not all of us can afford a single-family home."

Like many of my colleagues, I was lucky enough to find a second job to subsidize my work in the legislature. But the fact remains that low legislative pay makes it nearly impossible for young people to step up and run for office. The capitol building doesn't come close to reflecting the diversity of our state. The obvious, though unpopular, solution is to pay legislators an appropriate salary. No one should ever run for the state legislature to get rich, but perhaps serving in the legislature should no longer be a privilege reserved for those who can afford it. In the meantime, as Norm said, we'll get what we pay for.

30

Someone Else's Boss

About a year after my first legislative session wrapped up, I had a chance to Zoom with some of the students who benefited from Connecticut's free community college program. The Higher Education Committee was now fighting to renew the program's funding, and students shared stories about how the assistance had changed their lives. Izzy, enrolled at Northwestern Community College, told me that attending community college without going into debt had allowed her to save money toward a future law degree. Lilia, a student at Three Rivers Community College, said that her family hadn't been able to save for college due to the medical bills associated with her mother's breast cancer treatment. The free tuition opportunity made community college "a no-brainer," and she looked forward to becoming an English teacher. Christopher, who attended Housatonic Community College, called the program a "lifesaver," allowing him to spend less time worrying about tuition costs and more time focusing on coursework.

I think about Izzy, Lilia, and Christopher often. I think about our campaign interns who turned over their lives to licking envelopes and knocking on doors so that we could create a program like this. I wonder if I'll let them down when I decide to step back.

As I write this, I don't plan to run for reelection again in 2022. I've learned so much in this job, and I think I've helped to build a slightly better future for our state. But after two terms, I'm ready to say goodbye to my 100,000 bosses. I didn't run for office because I thought I was the only or best person to represent these seven suburbs. I ran because I thought it was time for a change. Now, it's time for change once again. I believe that government works best when new voices and different perspectives enter the caucus room or the committee hearing, challenging the conventional wisdom that too often stifles good policy.

On the night that Jack and I hosted our dorm-room fundraiser, I stopped being a regular college student and instead started to think and talk like a politician. Since that moment, my role as a senator has consumed every aspect of my life. I think about my 100,000 bosses from the moment I wake up until the moment I go to sleep. And I can't imagine a cooler first job. But now I'm ready to live with the person I love, stress less about what's printed in the Letter to the Editor section, and control my own calendar. You could say I'm looking forward to being someone else's boss.

My unlikely job as a twenty-two-year-old lawmaker taught me that politicians still answer to the people. Underdog candidates can pull off a win, and sometimes they can even impact public policy. I may be stepping away from politics for the moment, but I can't imagine leaving for good. In the meantime, I look forward to calling up my future state senator and making my voice heard.

Acknowledgments

I laughed out loud when Esther Newberg called and suggested that I write a book. For one thing, COVID-19 was tearing through Connecticut, and I was on the phone for twelve hours a day with constituents and colleagues. Plus, I wasn't sure that anyone outside of Fairfield County, Connecticut, cared about my experience running for office. But Esther isn't the type of agent or person to take no for an answer. Katie's brother Nick Cion, a writer whose wittiness I envy, coached me through drafting an outline. And to my surprise, Jofie Ferrari-Adler and the team at Avid Reader Press decided that publishing this unusual story might encourage other young people to take a leap of faith and pursue public service.

But the person who took the biggest chance on this book is my editor, Carolyn Kelly. Throughout the drafting process, I found it easy to forget that Carolyn is my age and that this is her very first book. Over the course of an unusual and challenging year, she and I passed drafts back and forth, working to put together a story that might resonate with our generation. We brainstormed about how to make legislative mechanics exciting, and she read each new version with an astounding attention to detail.

Katie has been along for the ride since the moment I made the crazy decision to run for office, and at nearly every critical juncture over the last few years she has reminded me of the person I am outside of politics. Throughout this process, nothing was more nerve-racking than showing my first draft to her, as I've quietly envied her natural talent as a writer since reading her columns in our high school newspaper. Katie told me to stop referencing *The West Wing* and insisted that I use the Oxford comma. But more importantly, she hugged me and told me that she was prouder than ever. She knows me better than my 99,999 other bosses, and her edits helped ensure that this book was more honest than any stump speech or campaign flyer had been.

Shortly after the 2020 election, I went away for a week or so and tried to pull together everything I had drafted into a narrative that made some sense. Alex Romanowicz worked even harder than he usually does to keep things running smoothly in Hartford, and friends and family weighed in with helpful feedback. Jack Lynch reviewed each chapter to make sure our recollections from the campaign trail matched, and Jack Aldrich helped me think through what distinguishes his generation (millennials) from the youngest set of voters (Gen Z). Liam Treanor reminded me to add some humor, and Kevin Alvarez insisted that I paint a more vivid picture of the personalities we had encountered together. Elizabeth and Maddy, my best friends since elementary school, helped me imagine what the cover might eventually look like, and Big Bob convinced me not to include too many swear words. My brother David dedicated his scarce time to helping me think through issues big and small, from which legislative fights were worth highlighting to how this book should end. Joe Quinn was nice enough to take my calls and offer the legal advice that allowed this book to become a reality. Marty, Bob, and my colleagues-turned-friends in Hartford gave me the push I needed to write a story that provided an inside look at our work under the capitol dome.

Thank you to the awesome Simon & Schuster team, including Amanda Mulholland, Elizabeth Hubbard, Annie Craig, Jordan Rodman, Gil Cruz, Meredith Vilarello, Alison Forner, Math Monahan, Sydney Newman, Yvette Grant, Brigid Black, and Kyle Kabel.

This unlikely story would not have been possible without groups like the ReSisters, 203Action, and seven DTCs that worked so hard to flip this district. I feel so lucky to have mentors who are generous with their time and wisdom, including Jim Himes, Chris Murphy, Bob Duff, and more. And of course, thank you to the student interns and volunteers who were the heart of our team. I can't wait to see what each of you accomplish next.

Much like running a campaign or serving in the state Senate, I learned that writing a book is a team effort. I'm grateful for everyone on this team—those who are mentioned above and those who aren't. To those who I've poked fun at, please know how much I respect and love everyone who helped turn this dorm-room pipe dream into a reality. Your kindness and intelligence have pushed me to work harder, especially when the prospect of writing a few pages at the end of a long day seemed impossible. If we manage to inspire one person to roll up their sleeves and run for office, I think it will have been worth it.

About the Author

In 2018, **Will Haskell** was elected to represent seven towns, including his hometown of Westport, in the Connecticut State Senate. Just a few months after graduating from college, he and his roommate-turned-campaign-manager unseated a Republican incumbent who had been in the legislature for longer than Will had been alive. Their campaign activated an army of young volunteers who were energized by the fight to end gun violence, and together they broke a tie in the Senate by flipping the district blue. In the Senate, Will serves as chair of the Transportation Committee and the vice chair of the Government Administration and Elections Committee. He spent his first term focusing on college affordability, transportation improvements, and voting rights. In 2019, he helped create Connecticut's free community college program, so that every high school graduate has an opportunity to pursue a degree. He lives in Westport, Connecticut, and is still dating his lab partner from high school physics. *100,000 First Bosses* is his first book.